YOU A
BACKPACK

THE SECRETS OF HOW TO TRAVEL
THE WORLD; ADVICE, TIPS AND
TRICKS FOR TRAVELERS

BY VICTORIA ROBERTS

Copyright © 2019 Victoria Roberts

All Rights Reserved
Kindle Edition

All rights reserved. Without limiting the rights under the copyright reserved above, no part of this publication may be reproduced, stored in, or introduced into a retrieval system, or transmitted in any form or by any means (electronic, mechanical, photocopying, recording, or otherwise) without prior written permission.

For permission requests, please contact: info@youandyourbackpack.com

While every effort has been made to ensure the accuracy and legitimacy of the references, referrals, and links (collectively "Links") presented in this eBook, Victoria Roberts is not responsible or liable for broken Links or missing or fallacious information at the Links. Any Links in this eBook to a specific product, process, website, or service do not constitute or imply an endorsement by Victoria Roberts of same, or its producer or provider. The views and opinions contained at any Links do not necessarily express or reflect those of Victoria Roberts.

For more tips and tricks check out
youandyourbackpack.com

For my long-suffering Dad, who has bailed me out, pepped me up and patched me together more times than I can count. He can certainly blame a grey hair or ten on me and my adventures.

He's travelled every one of these moments with me, albeit from his sofa.

Table of Contents

Introduction 1

Section 1 The Prep 3

Chapter 1 Planning an Itinerary 4

Chapter 2 Packing 13

Chapter 3 Admin 24

Chapter 4 Financial Planning..................................... 28

Section 2.. 35

Section 2 The Road.. 35

Chapter 5 Life on the Road 37

Chapter 6 Staying Sane 51

Chapter 7 Staying Safe 61

Chapter 8 Staying Healthy... 84

Chapter 9 Money 95

Chapter 10 Technology 109

Section 3 The Return... 119

Chapter 11 Settling Back Home 120

About the Author 132

One Last Thing….. 133

INTRODUCTION

Over the years, I have made about every travel mistake possible. I have been mugged at gunpoint, stranded penniless, lost, hospitalized, drugged and a little bit kidnapped. I have consistently been in the wrong place at the wrong time, surviving through political coups, hurricanes, flash floods and pretty much everything in between.

For those who have never gone "'travelling", it can be a daunting idea. Contemplating doing it alone, however, can be nothing short of terrifying. There are a thousand questions, reasons not to, and seemingly insurmountable obstacles that can make the idea of travelling stay just that, an idea.

Think of this book as a guidebook to everywhere. It's packed full of travel tips and tricks; from budgeting to bribery, health to homesickness and, most importantly, how you can stay safe, not scared. Every lesson in this book is a piece of advice that I've found out the hard way, and one that you can learn without doing the legwork.

I'll show you that not only is it possible, but, with a bit

of advice, prep and planning, it can be a life-changing rollercoaster from breath-taking highs, seeing the pyramids and dancing in waterfalls, to (retrospectively) funny lows, like coming down with explosive diarrhoea on a 10-hour bus ride in Ecuador or running away from a hungry Komodo dragon in Indonesia.

I am thirty years old and have devoted most of the last twelve years to packing up, travelling the world, semi-settling and then doing it all again, filling up two passports with stamps, almost all of it happily alone. I don't have a house or an expensive car, but I have so many memories and life-changing experiences from across the world, having dipped into other cultures (some more successfully than others) and made lifelong friends from just about everywhere. Travel changes something inside you, broadens the mind and, for me anyway, has created a beautiful, insatiable wanderlust that I hope I am never cured of.

SECTION 1

THE PREP

Preparation is an ever-important part of a successful trip. A little planning can mean a smooth-running adventure that doesn't involve being lost and penniless in the bad area of town in monsoon season. While the many areas of preparation can seem daunting, together we will talk through finances, itinerary planning, what to pack, and many other tips and tricks that will make the difference between a travel-blog-worthy venture and a trip to Bolivia in the middle of winter with no warm clothes, as I subjected myself to when I was eighteen, on my first jaunt away from home.

CHAPTER 1

PLANNING AN ITINERARY

Itinerary planning is always a tough one to advise on, as it is so individual to a person's interests, budget, level of travel fear, season and length of trip.

What Do You Like Doing?

I would seriously sit down and think, with complete honesty, about what you would like to get out of your trip. While some people would love tubing high on mushrooms in Laos and dancing till sunrise at full moon parties in Thailand, others prefer hiking, history or home comforts. Both ends of the spectrum and everything in the middle can be easily found, but some places do lend themselves to more of one thing than the other. Make a list of what kind of activities you enjoy at home or on holidays now – some travellers have a romantic notion that as soon as they go away, they will suddenly transform into a cultural warrior who will spend all day learning about history and studying local wood carvings, when in reality they would rather be having a massage or going to the pub.

If you like nature and *actually* go hiking (not just like the idea of it and actually watch four hours of Netflix in bed instead), then maybe the hills of Patagonia are for you. There are no prizes for what you achieve travelling, and unless you plan a trip to fit your interests, rather than what you think you "should" be doing to "find yourself", you will most likely end up being unhappy and changing your plans anyway.

What's Your Budget?

Some countries in the world are obviously cheaper than others, and this has to be a very real consideration when choosing destinations. While travel can be very cheap if you are careful (more on that later), places like Australia, parts of Europe, and the USA can be awfully expensive for long-term trips. Work out how much money you will have saved for the amount of time you want to travel for and work out a daily budget. Even if you are not so cash-strapped, it's still important to have a general idea of what you have to spend each day, meaning you know which days to eat local and when you can splash out on a nice hotel room with a big white bed and fluffy towels. I can tell you, jumping in a swimming pool once in a while feels like heaven when you've been roughing it.

For those on an extremely tight budget, South East Asia is normally a great option. Think Thailand, Cambodia, Laos, Vietnam, Thailand, Malaysia and Indonesia. Dirt cheap and very easy for first-time travellers, lots of backpackers to meet doing the same thing as you and great overland transport so no need for expensive and rigid internal flights. There's masses of culture here, you can easily get away from the throngs of backpackers should you so desire, the weather's stunning and it's easy to get by with English. For those still wanting dirt-cheap Asia but who are fed up with the full-moon crowd, India, Nepal and Sri Lanka are sufficiently off the backpacker beaten path to ensure you won't see too many tequila shots and bad suntans.

Central and South America are, again, a great option for budget travel, although a little bit harder to get around for those of us that don't speak Español. A few phrases will get you far, though, and most of the backpacker trail hotspots will cater for English-speaking travellers. Colombia, Ecuador, Peru, Bolivia, Nicaragua and Guatemala are all cheap as chips and offer history, culture, extreme sports and great nightlife. Argentina, Brazil, Costa Rica, Panama and Mexico will set you back a few Pesos more but are still amazing options.

Europe is another popular destination; with an Interrail pass to sort out between-stop transport, it can be easy to plan and maybe a little more similar to home than throwing yourself feet first into a culture shock. The history and beauty of Europe are staggering; however, the prices are, too, especially in the capitals. If you're on a budget, head over to Eastern Europe for a little more bang for your buck.

Australia, New Zealand, the UK and the USA are definitely not budget destinations but are very easy to travel: English speaking, with the food and comforts of home. For those more nervous about being too far from a proper hairdresser or anxious about a language barrier, they are amazing destinations and offer awesome scenery and countless things to do. Just make sure your budget can handle it before you bankrupt yourself in Brisbane.

Level of Fear

Going travelling for the first time, especially alone, *is* scary. But there are certain things you can do to control your level of stress. Certain destinations lend themselves to comfort, just as others do to danger. If you're nervous, I'd recommend not throwing yourself in the deep end right at the beginning. I think Thailand is a perfect place to start; you are guaranteed to meet people, and there are lots of options for tours and established travel routes. It's not necessarily the most authentic destination anymore, unless you can manage to get off the beaten track, but it's safe and cheap and great fun.

As a single traveller, especially as a girl, some countries are just more dangerous than others, and your appetite for mugging, etc. does have to be a serious consideration when itinerary choosing. I used to not put much thought into this, thinking that I could just be careful anywhere, and you can, but after a small kidnapping in Venezuela and getting mugged at gunpoint at an ATM in mainland Honduras, I have decided there are enough slightly safer countries in the world to travel to, and I no longer feel the need to push those boundaries to prove some sort of point. I recently spent six weeks in South Africa, and it was trouble free, but equally, there were a fair few murders while I was there. Decide on the level of crime you personally feel comfortable with and pick destinations in line with it.

When to Go

This is important. If you have fixed dates already, then pick destinations around them. If you have your heart set on certain places, then try and work on a plan to see them when they shine. While you can save money with off-peak travel, find out the extent of the seasons before you travel. Monsoon seasons can shut hotels for a few months of the year, dreams of cocktails in bikinis can be shattered by typhoons, and some people might not appreciate trying to meditate in an Indian temple while it's 50°C outside. Remember that the seasons are the opposite in the southern hemisphere, and give each place a quick Google to find optimal times to visit. Think about any festivals or special events you might want to go to, too. Where do I want to be for Christmas? Rio Carnival is in February, you can only see the Northern Lights in winter, everything shuts for August in Paris – you get the gist.

To Book or Not to Book

So now you have picked a destination, you have a rough budget and you know roughly when you're going. The next step is to get booking! Search around for cheap flights using comparison websites, try and book well in advance, and try lots of combinations of dates and arrival cities for the best deals. If you can get your big flight sorted, separately booked low-cost carriers can zip you about very cheaply once you're vaguely in the right place.

I like to book flights with lots of segments on one

ticket, that way if the first leg is delayed, the airlines will always rearrange your travel to your final destination and cover the cost. Just make sure you leave plenty of time for connections; terminal changes, complicated airport layouts and security checks can often make for a stressful nightmare otherwise.

Personally, I always like to have somewhere to stay booked for at least the night I arrive. Long plane journeys can be hell, and the last thing you want to be doing when you arrive is traipsing around a humid city with your backpack, desperately trying to find somewhere to lay your weary head. There's plenty of time to explore later. For me, that first night is about getting in, getting to a safe, clean hotel, having a shower and getting some good rest.

For the most part, after that first night, I rarely book anything in advance, the exception being if I'm attending a festival or it's New Year's Eve, etc. The beauty of travel lies in not overplanning. While I always have an idea of towns I'd like to visit or cool activities along my route, I like to leave the details to fill in themselves, depending on whom I meet, what I'm enjoying at the time and exactly what mood I'm in that day. The sheer freedom of doing exactly what you feel like is somewhat constricted with overplanning and strict itineraries.

Another good point is to make sure you don't overstretch. Trying to cross the length of South America in four weeks is either not going to happen or you'll rush so much along the way you'll never really have time to absorb the places you are in. It's always much better to spend more time in each place than rush about, spending most of your precious time on an array of buses, planes and trains.

If you're feeling the travel nerves and simply can't imagine what you're going to do with yourself all day and having mental images of spending three months entirely by yourself, I highly recommend booking something structured for the first few weeks. A Spanish course in your first two weeks of Colombia will mean you will meet people and have a base, and it will help you flourish for the rest of your trip. Similarly, some volunteering, a yoga or scuba diving course, Thai boxing lessons or a week's cooking class can achieve the same end. By the time it's over, you'll feel more adjusted to your environment and have the confidence to start veering off solo.

An organised, overland tour can offer the same structure. There are different options based on budget, age or activity levels, and these can be a good option for more nervous travellers. I have done a couple of these tours, and personally, I find them rather constricting, but it could definitely be a great option for easing yourself into life on the road, especially for the first couple of weeks, and then leaving the rest of your trip open to go solo.

CHAPTER 2
PACKING

The beauty of travelling is the freedom. If you weigh yourself down with two suitcases full of high heels, frisbees, a hammock and your own water purification system, you will kick yourself when trying to lug them up to hostel bedrooms, dragging them along a beach to find a bungalow, or paying extra on every form of transport. You really don't need to bring more than the bare essentials because guess what, they have shops wherever you are going, and if you need something, you can buy it! Personally, I like to travel very light, with enough clothes that can go from day to night and a few essential beauty items.

The first time I went travelling, I fell into the typical "backpacker" trap. Trousers that unzipped into shorts, special hiking sandals, my own mosquito net… I think I even brought a foldable hat-in-a-bag. You have to realise that you are going to normal places. You will want to wear the same type of clothes you have at home because they suit you and you feel comfortable in them. Wearing high-performance hiking gear is only good on hikes; the rest of the time, you will be in bars and restaurants and taking Insta-worthy pics on beautiful beaches. Take clothes that you would enjoy doing those things in.

Think about the climate! If you will be travelling through a few different types of weather, just plan for the first one; you can pick up warm gear/bikinis on the way and hand the rest over to the next traveller in need.

What to Pack

Everyone's packing list will be different, depending on destination, personal preference and willpower, but we will go ahead and discuss the basics, and then you can decide what's right for you. Then remove half the stuff!

1. Your luggage. You will read blog posts that profess carry-on luggage is the way to go. While this is probably true, I'd rather have checked-in luggage and a few more creature comforts. I've always opted for a comfy, padded backpack as there have been plenty of times that hard luggage just wouldn't have been as convenient for stuffing things in various compartments, or I've been walking half a mile along a beach to reach

accommodation, or along a gravel track, and wheels just wouldn't have cut it. Equally, there have been plenty of times where a perfectly concreted road made me loathe my sweat-inducing pack, cursing while I wished for wheels. Consider just how remote you're going to be on your trip and make the right choice for you. Guaranteed at some point or another, you will long for the option that's not the one which currently holds all your worldly possessions, but such is the traveller's curse. If you can find a light, comfy backpack *with* wheels, then the road is your oyster.

2. Get a good carry-on bag. This has to be something you can use as a day bag on the road – think beach towels, guidebooks, water bottles – but also one that you can wear easily while you have your main bag on. You can always go for the back-and-front backpack look when you're schlepping around with both. I don't recommend a day bag that gets zipped to the outside of your main backpack, though. I once had one of these unzipped and stolen on the way to the airport in Bangkok, and it didn't make for a happy journey home. In fact, it meant being penniless and hungry in Bahrain airport on a seven-hour stopover and

begging for train fare at Heathrow to get me home. You need a small purse or wallet for your bank cards and money, but more on this in the next chapter. Keep all of your important and expensive items with you in your carry on, through planes, trains, hotel receptions, etc. These are your essentials and must be stuck to you like glue. Lost clothes and toiletries can be easily replaced at a street market or local mall, lost passports and bank cards not so much.

3. Packing cubes are fantastic for separating underwear, toiletries, dirty laundry and electronics so your bag doesn't become a jumbled nightmare. These are cheap and make a huge difference when you're living life out of a bag.

4. Obviously, you need a few changes of clothes, but less is honestly more. Cheap laundry options are always available wherever backpackers seem to congregate, and no one really dresses up. Think shorts for daytime and shorts for nighttime! A few t-shirts and cute tops. Maybe one sundress or shirt and long pants that can go either way, just in case you go somewhere a little fancy for dinner. Chuck in a couple (yes, just two) bikinis or swim

shorts, and job done. If you're heading to a colder climate, you will obviously need more layers. I normally wear a pair of jeans on the plane for any chilly nights, cold movie theatres or horse-riding, maybe? I also like to pack a comfy hoodie. I guess it's a luxury item, but I love a snuggle, and planes are cold.

5. You really don't need many shoes. I have definitely been guilty of taking too many in the past. Once I counted my shoes in Vietnam, and I had seven pairs – so unnecessary. I normally wear a pair of sneakers on the plane. Make sure they are versatile ones that you'd be happy walking around town in but could also wear on a hike, and bring a pair of flip-flops. I normally bring one pair of ballet pump-type shoes in case I end up in a real restaurant or nightclub, but that is honestly all you need. Heels are heavy and a waste of time. You'll mostly be dancing on beaches anyway!

6. Bring a sarong or buy one on the way! This is so multi-function it's essential: a blanket on a cold plane, somewhere to sit on the beach, a shoulder wrap in a temple, a pillow, and maybe, just maybe, as an actual sarong.

7. Protect your sleep. One thing I never leave

home without is my little sleep pack. From overnight trains to noisy snorers in shared dorm rooms, some earplugs, an eye mask and a small inflatable neck pillow will make for a happy traveller the following morning.

8. A travel towel will go a long way when hostel towels are for rent or just disgusting. It is also great for the beach.

9. Prescription medications if you need any. These can be a pain to replace, so take enough for your trip. Grab any malaria meds you need, too. I normally carry some Imodium for emergencies (just accept that this is going to happen at some point) and maybe some general painkillers for the odd headache/hangover, but that's about it. You honestly don't need a big first aid kit. If you get ill, there are hospitals and pharmacies everywhere, and you can bet it's cheaper than home, anyway.

10. Toiletries: take the very basics to get you through. I always take bits of makeup but never the whole shebang. My hair straighteners stay firmly at home, as does my perfume, manicure kit and exfoliator. Shampoo, conditioner and body wash can be

topped up on the road, and some sun cream, a (non-electric) toothbrush, razor, hairbrush, lady's hygiene items, tweezers and some deodorant, and I'm pretty much good. I would throw in some condoms for protection for the more intimate moments; this is something not worth skimping on! I have to be really strict with myself with toiletries; they are bulky and heavy, but once you start practising a very pared-down beauty routine, you get used to it, and it's amazingly freeing.

11. Bring a small padlock. Many hostels have lockers to keep your things safe. Always lock your locker when you're not there or use a safe if available. There's nothing worse than being robbed by a fellow traveller or someone working in the hotel.

12. Your gadgets. Get a great smartphone – the best part is you probably already have one. This is your world: your camera (unless you're really into photography and are planning on bringing a huge DSLR), your music (download enough for when you can't stream), your torch, your library (I use it as a Kindle and therefore never have to carry heavy books), your alarm clock, your journal (there are some

amazing journal apps), your lifeline for maps, guidebooks, translations, staying in touch and mindless browsing. Unless you are a serious travel blogger or run a business from your laptop, you really don't need one when travelling. They are bulky and heavy and mostly unused when it comes down to it. If you suddenly desperately need a real computer for something your phone fails you on, there are always internet cafes dotted around which are cheap and easy. Buy a good case for your phone so you can drop it and dunk it. (I like Lifeproof.) Get your phone insured if you're the type that might lose it. Be wary about bringing your old one; normally the batteries aren't the best, and you'll just yearn for the one you have sitting at home. Talking about batteries, a small but powerful power bank is absolutely worth the investment so you can keep charged up on the move and through long transits. Take a travel adapter for at least your first destination; you can buy more along the way as you go. You need a pair of headphones but not huge over-the-ear monsters. While they might look cool in normal life, when you're travelling they take up a huge amount of room when not on your head. You are not an audio engineer, and you can cope with ear pods or the like.

13. A few extra bits like sunglasses, contacts or glasses if you need them and a baseball cap for sunny days, and you're done! Also, always carry a pen in your carry-on for filling out landing cards!

What Not to Pack

You really need to take a lot less than you think. Be ruthless. Know that you can do laundry often on the road; no, you don't need a penknife unless you use one at home. Lay out what you think you need ahead of time and edit it before your trip; take out anything that you don't absolutely have to have. You can do this on the road, too. It will soon become obvious if you're not using something. Don't be afraid to thin out your things; give them to other travellers or send them home by post if they're expensive. The compromises you make while packing will pay you back tenfold when you're rooting around in a bottomless backpack and lugging it on and off trains and buses.

You really don't need a money belt. Carry small amounts of cash and be aware of your stuff and surroundings. The same goes for a bag lock. They are big, bulky and expensive, and there is never a convenient pole to attach it to. You should stay with your bag when you're out and about, anyway; you are a snail, and it is your shell. Water purification tablets are only for jungle explorers and serious hikers. Sleeping bag liners take up space and are rarely used; guess what, bed bugs will just get into the material, and then you will take them along with you on your trip!

Most things bought at a camping store don't have much place in normal-style backpacking. You will wish you hadn't wasted your money or valuable bag space which you could fill up with a few extra clothes, a hoodie or souvenirs.

Actually Packing

So, the (exciting) time has come to actually pack your rucksack. Use your packing cubes to separate items into categories for easy retrieval, then start by putting the heaviest things in the bottom so you're not too unstable when it's on your back. Get to know your backpack, and use all the little pockets to stash stuff you might need to get to in a rush. Try not to fill your backpack to the absolute brim. Once you stock up on shampoo, etc. on arrival or buy a souvenir, you won't be able to close it! Remember to place any valuables in your carry-on but no liquids or aerosols in containers bigger than 100 ml. Pop your sleep kit in your carry-on to catch a nap on the plane. Finish your masterpiece by tying a distinctive ribbon or tag around your bag so you can easily pick it out on an airport carousel or worse, from a pile of identical-looking backpacks when you've just completed a 13-hour bus ride.

CHAPTER 3

ADMIN

There are plenty of small things you can do before you go to make your trip run more smoothly. The good news is you can make a start on these well in advance, meaning when you're busy seeing temples and sipping Pina Coladas, you won't have worries about money, visas or where your mail is ending up. The more time and effort you put in ahead of time, the more pain-free travel you can look forward to in the coming months!

Paperwork

The cloud is your friend, a central storage for important documents that you can access from anywhere, even if you lose your phone and all seems lost. If you don't have one already, create a Google Drive or Dropbox account. Take copies of your passport, insurance details, itineraries and emergency contact numbers and save them to it. While you have your passport out, check the expiry date – it needs to be valid for at least six months from the date you plan to enter your last country, but it's better to have more for safety. Check you also have enough empty pages; some of those obscure entry stamps take a whole page!

Make sure you print out your flight tickets, even though you have them online. Some airports won't allow you in the front door without them. Make sure you can also show proof of onward travel, many countries won't allow you to enter without an exit ticket, and it's better to have one of these even if you're actually planning on travelling to your next destination overland. Find a fully refundable fare and cancel it once you arrive, it would be a shame to get through all this prep and then get turned away at the check-in counter!

Take some spare passport photos with you for random visas or multi-day passes; photographers often charge a fortune when they know tourists have no option. Make sure you check the entry requirements for each country you're planning to visit; visa wait times can often be long, and it's better to get ahead of the game on this one. I once bribed my way into Malaysia with cigarettes as I didn't have the cash on me to buy the visa – not recommended; do your homework instead.

Life at Home

Although it might seem like time stands still while you're away, life will tick on without you. Make sure you set all your recurring bills to direct debit so you won't forget to pay them while you're playing in waterfalls. Cancel any subscriptions you won't be using while you're away; the cost of your cable package, gin of the month club, gym membership and cellular plan will add up to being able to scuba dive, bungee jump or spend a week in a bungalow in Bali.

Reroute your mail to a PO Box or a trusted friend or relative. Not much of great importance gets sent via mail these days, so just make sure all your bank and credit card statements are online, and get them to give you a heads up if there's anything important.

Make sure you cancel any cleaners/gardeners, arrange for house sitters or, better yet, pack up your place to save money on bills while you're away. Making a plan will mean it's easier to leave, knowing everything is secure and sorted.

Health

Go to the doctor well ahead of time, get a full check up and tell him anything that has been niggling you. Tell the doctor the countries you will be travelling to and get the relevant immunisations or malaria medication. This is better done sooner rather than later: sometimes multiple doses are required over time, and the vaccinations can make you feel a little sick for a few days – not the best when you are trying to pack and plan a leaving party!

Make sure you get to the dentist well ahead of time, too. Get a full check up and make sure everything is sorted out so you don't end up trying to get a filling from a questionable dentist in the Bahamas. (I had to have the whole thing re-done in London months later.)

Get some decent travel insurance for anything that might go wrong along the way. Those scooters in Asia have a nasty habit of ejecting tourists off them after a couple too many beers, and even Asian hospitals get extremely pricey very quickly. Travel insurance can be bought for a few dollars a day and can cover anything from your precious cell phone to emergency evacuations in a disaster. Buy it; hopefully, you'll never need to use it.

CHAPTER 4

FINANCIAL PLANNING

Saving

Saving money for travels can be a sticky issue and probably one of the main reasons why many people don't go. Over the years, so many of my friends at home have told me how lucky I am to be able to afford to travel or how they never could. In reality, it just comes down to priorities. I have never had designer clothes, the best car or latest smartphone; nor have I wanted them. I don't have many possessions, and the only thing I collect is passport stamps. These are choices I have been happy to make, and it honestly can be that easy.

Firstly, open a new savings account. This is your new travelling fund and can't be dipped into to highlight your hair or buy football tickets! Set up a direct debit for just after you get paid straight into your savings account with whatever you can afford, be it $1,000 or $50. If you wait till the end of the month and see what's left to save, often the sad answer is zero.

Try and cut out any unnecessary spending in your life. Maybe cancel your gym membership and go for a run instead; do you need Netflix, Cable *and* Hulu or could you cope with just one for a few months? Try and analyse all your monthly outgoings and put any savings directly into your new travel fund. Every time you choose to cook instead of going out for dinner or getting take-out, top up the travel fund. Each time you avoid the mall and wear a dress you already own instead of buying a new one, top up the travel fund. You'll be surprised how quickly it runs up, and it's so gratifying.

You can also have a look around you and see if a garage sale or an eBay purge might be beneficial. Think about moving back with your parents for a few months just before you set off. Imagine all that money spent on rent and bills going straight into your savings account! Maybe it's worth spending time with mum and dad, suddenly?

If these changes aren't enough, consider working extra shifts or getting a part-time second job to top up that fund. Even if it's just for a few months, it will be worth the sacrifice.

Budgeting

We talked briefly about budgets when we looked at

planning our itinerary, but let's dive in a bit deeper.

Of course, there are going to be some initial costs, booking the expensive flights and maybe a new bag, immunisations, etc. With those taken into account, you can start to look at a daily budget. There are many apps and budget tools to keep you on track, but a bit of planning and knowing a rough daily spend can really mean the difference between happy travels and backpack bankrupt.

How you travel is going to make a huge difference, and this is something to decide up front. Infinity pools and internal flights don't come cheap in any region, so set your expectations straight. Do you want to eat out every night? Are you prepared to eat local? Are you a flashpacker or a shoestring budget kind of person? Drawing up a realistic budget of how you are prepared to live life on the road involves asking yourself these questions. Maybe you'd prefer a more luxurious standard of living for a shorter time period, or maybe you're prepared to skip the Singapores and Sydneys of the world for the Philippine beach huts and hostels in Guatemala. Living off $10 a day is possible, but not everyone wants to stay in dirty hostels in the wrong end of town and eat a diet of straight street food. Whatever your travel style is, be honest about it now, because the trouble starts if it's not in your budget but the occasional four-star hotel ends up creeping in. Google guidelines for your specific destination and come up with a daily figure that suits the kind of lifestyle you want on the road.

Think about any specific activities you would like to do. A scuba diving qualification or a helicopter ride over the Grand Canyon should be budgeted in ahead of time as these are big outlays. Are you planning to book any internal flights, or can you take cheaper ground transport between destinations? If you love to shop, then factor it in. Personally, I don't often buy souvenirs. I take lots of photos and make lots of memories but really buy only a postcard in the places I visit. Souvenirs take up precious bag space and when you get home gather dust on a shelf. By all means, buy stuff if you will genuinely adore it once the travel fever has worn off, but for me, it's not really worth it.

Also remember to factor in any bills you have at home, any subscription services that you can't or don't want to cancel, or credit card payments that will be coming out of your account while you're away.

Once you have an idea of all these costs, you will have a rough idea of the money you need to save and what you can spend every day. Divide it up into rough categories such as food, accommodation and fun; then you will know if you're on track when you choose hotels and restaurants. It might be a good idea to split it up into sections if you are heading to different areas of the world where costs differ significantly. A hotel in Bali will never cost the same as one in Paris.

Lastly, make sure you have a bit of reserve cash. You never know what might happen when you're away, whether it's emergency dental work, a missed flight, or your roof falling in at home. It's always best to have some money in a slush fund for the unknown. You also need to make sure you have something put aside for when you get back. It will be a long month to wait for your first paycheck back in the real world if your bank statement reads a row of zeros.

Spending

Throughout your trip, thousands will be coming out of your bank account and flowing into various currencies around the world. Nobody uses traveller's cheques anymore, carrying large amounts of cash is not the most secure thing ever, so using cards is the answer. You would be shocked at the number of tiny retailers that take card nowadays, and you can still use an ATM to get cash out for a little walking-around money. Most banks and credit cards charge for foreign transactions, so find one that doesn't. My favourite is Revolut. It's a simple, app-based, top-up account which you can refill and spend from in almost any currency with no exchange or transaction fees. They will even replace your card wherever you are in the world within two days. There is a great analytics feature that lets you see how much money you're spending and on what, and daily budget reminders whenever you spend. There are quite a few similar alternatives on the market, but whatever you choose, please don't just use your normal debit card. Even if they don't charge you fees, they will give you an extremely unfavourable exchange rate, and you will end up wasting lots of your hard-saved travel fund on making the bank richer. It's nice to have a little local currency to get a taxi or bus when you land, but whatever you do, never change currency at the airport; the rates they give are daylight robbery.

It's always good to have backup options in regard to money when abroad. I use my Revolut card on a day-to-day basis, and I also have a credit card with a high limit in case of emergencies (like a hurricane, rather than a round of tequila). I also carry my debit card, again, just in case. You never know when an ATM will eat your card (in Peru), the chip will get damaged and not work (South Africa), you will get pickpocketed (Colombia) or you will lose it on a night out (about 20 different occasions all over the damn world). Keep the cards in separate places, and don't take them all out at the same time as it kind of defeats the purpose.

SECTION 2

THE ROAD

So, you've planned, you've packed, probably repacked, and you've got yourself to the other side of the world. What on earth do you do now?

The first time I went travelling, a fresh-faced 18-year-old who thought I was worldlier than I was, I naively chose to buy a one-way ticket to Ecuador. When the plane landed, I was the last person to get off. I was sitting in my seat paralysed by fear and hoping that if I stayed where I was, it would turn around and take me back home to London. Eventually, I negotiated my way into a taxi and straight to a hotel I had booked for the first few nights. I spent the next three days ordering room service, reading every book in my bag and gazing mindlessly at Spanish TV. I couldn't imagine moving on, so I went downstairs to extend my stay another couple of days, but to my horror, the hotel was fully booked. I took a deep breath, consulted my Lonely Planet and got a taxi to the nearest hostel. Suddenly, it was ok. I was surrounded by other travellers who were going out to restaurants, seeing cool sights, going out dancing, and shockingly, had survived it all. The best thing about it was that I was invited. Within an hour, I had taken off my money belt (never to be worn again, to this day) and jumped on a bus. I went on a night out and, somewhere along the way, found some confidence. I travelled with this same lovely group of people for a few days, and by the time I moved on to my next city on my own, I didn't even blink.

It's scary to jump in at the deep end, but I promise it's not as bad as you think. After all, this is meant to be fun! This is the moment for which you've spent hours scouring blogs for advice, jealously gazing at Instagram, and scrimped and saved your pennies. It's a pretty daunting feeling to be out of your depth and a hell of a long way from your comfort zone, months of nothing scheduled stretching in front of you, knowing no-one; it takes a beat to get into the swing of it.

In the next section, we'll talk about how you can stay safe, stay sane and get the most out of your travel experience, keeping fit, fun and thriving while you puddle jump through the world's jungles, mountains, beaches and, let's face it, bars.

CHAPTER 5

LIFE ON THE ROAD

Where to Stay

We've talked about booking somewhere for the first couple of nights to ease pre-travel panic and let you recover from your journey. But what's next? I like to mix it up a little along the way, varying different types of accommodation depending on location and my mood.

I spend most of my time in hostels. They are a great option for budget travel and a great place to meet other travellers and get tips and information about the local area. Accommodation in hostels can consist of dormitories (both same-sex and unisex), private single rooms and private double rooms. And they can be geared towards all traveller types: young, old, single, couples, male and female. Hostels are your bread and butter but do come in varying levels of comfort. Some make you feel like part of the family as soon as you walk in the door; in others, you hardly see a soul. Look at online reviews: hostelworld.com is a great site, and you can pick one nearby that suits what you're up for at the time. Some are definitely party zones; a few have strict curfews and rules; others have a kitchen where you can save money by cooking up a storm. Think about whether you can put up with sharing (and the snoring/amorous noises that come along with it) or whether you'd like some personal space. Some of the best hostels book up in advance, so make sure you make a reservation before you rock up.

If hostels are still breaking your budget, you can always try camping or couch surfing. Neither have practically appealed to me, as the former lacks the comfort I crave and the latter always seems like imposing and gives me nightmares of getting kidnapped. However, plenty of travellers swear by both, and it's up to you to decide whether you fancy giving either a try. Airbnb can offer home-like comforts with the convenience of a hotel, but for me, it is often a little lonely; it may be better for a couple or a group, but if it suits your travel style, then go for it!

Hotel options are usually a little pricier. I tend to dip into a nice(ish) hotel once a month or so for a night or two, and my budget is designed to reflect this. For me, it offers a little sanity break from the grubbiness which I often find myself surrounded by. A little bit of luxury and an hour in a real bath can recharge you for weeks, giving you fresh energy to tear forth on the path ahead. I will say, though, the more I pay for accommodation, the fewer people I seem to meet. I often stick to the lower end of the accommodation spectrum, even if my budget will allow for more, just to mix with similar-minded travellers and have a bit of fun.

Wherever you choose to stay, you have the freedom to move, chop and change, and feel out what's right for you. For most travellers, a happy combination of all the above is what they eventually settle on.

Getting Around

There are so many options when it comes to travelling between destinations, and it will mostly come down to your budget, time restrictions and comfort choices. Each destination will have different challenges and benefits. Night trains around Thailand and Vietnam, for example, are super cheap and comfortable, with your own bunk and cabin service, another upside being you are saving on a night's accommodation in the process. On the long stretches of road in South America, however, buses are your only real option. The winding, bumpy roads offer many a day (too risky at night) of staring out of the window in awe of stunning scenery. You could choose to rough it like a local and sit on a wooden bench, next to a giant, squirming bag of guinea pigs, for eight hours, like I did in Peru, or upgrade to a full Lazy Boy-style lounger with your own TV, which I did on every subsequent journey after the guinea pig incident.

In every big traveller hotspot, or even through your hostel reception, you can buy tickets of any description on to your next adventure. They will often conveniently package these up with ferries and transfers, so you can sit back, relax and get some sometimes-elusive rest. Make sure you keep your carry-on with your valuables on your person if you have to get separated from your main luggage. There are many horror stories about people losing all their worldly possessions while having a bus nap.

Generally, the more slowly you travel, the cheaper it is, but if you're flush with cash or short on time, then look at low-cost local airlines to get you from A to B. I once took a bus for a 36-hour journey from hell from Bangkok to Kuala Lumpur, Malaysia. On paper, it seemed like a great way to save money, but I didn't like the reality too much. However, a slow boat between Laos and northern Thailand was a lazy dream. Any way you go, you'll bump into an experience, but just decide what's right for you at the time.

Always shop around, low cost airlines can save you valuable time if you get a deal, but trains have to win as my favourite. Always taking you directly to the city centre, no security checks or checking in two hours ahead of time and a lot less tiring than the comparative flight. Every situation will be different, so check all your options before you buy.

At any border-crossing be extra vigilant about your bags. Double check them before you get close to immigration and never carry anything over for a friend. This means not trusting your taxi driver, tour guide or new travel-pal to watch your belongings and taking time to thoroughly check through, especially if they have been out of your sight for any reason. Drug smugglers prey on travellers and spending time in jail in a third world country would not be fun.

One of my more memorable travel calamities occurred on the return home from one of many trips to Thailand. I was a newbie traveller and had just come to the end of my first real backpacking adventure, accompanied by my older brother. I was returning home to start university, whilst he was continuing on to Indonesia, so when he asked if I could bring home a few souvenirs to lighten his load, I happily agreed. Turns out these souvenirs were throwing stars, numb chucks, and a small ornate sword (all destined for his wall, not for use). These items were bought in the open, from normal shops in touristy areas, and of course stashed safety in my hold luggage, it didn't really cross my mind they were illegal.

As my name echoed over the tannoy in the airport to report to security, my stomach was in knots of dread about what was to come. They had scanned my luggage and I got arrested for smuggling weapons. I was given no access to an interpreter and was left in a cell for 5 hours while the angry officers tried to make me sign a statement in Thai, luckily, I refused until the British Embassy were called. In the end they just let me go, and somewhat bemusingly, let me keep the weapons. I had of course missed my flight, but the lovely desk staff at the airport must have taken pity on the 18-year old, frightened mess of a girl that stood before them and rebooked my flight for free. Moral of the story: don't carry stupid things through borders or airports. Lesson learnt.

As for getting around town once you arrive, I tend to use a lot of public transport. Buses and metro services are often the most reliable way to dart about, not to mention the cheapest. You can always rent a car, but I find its normally a nightmare to park, and you're contending with the questionable driving practices in any given region. Uber is your friend and pops up in a surprising number of cities nowadays. Be careful if you are jumping into normal taxis or tuk-tuks, and always negotiate a price first so you don't get screwed at the other end.

Filling Your Days

Time and time again, I see backpackers who have come all the way to the other side of the world and then simply go to bars, restaurants and the mall. "Where's the nearest McDonalds?" is a popular phrase heard down Khao San Road, backpacker central in Bangkok. Well, good news for some, it's about 100m away, but why bother with all the effort of travelling if you're not going to really appreciate where you are?

Whenever I get to a new city, I spend time reading up on it (that's what long bus or train rides are for!) so I have a rough idea of any big must-do attractions in the area. You're not going to visit Paris without going to the Eiffel Tower, right? Speaking of which, it is best to hit these big tourist traps first thing. Wake up early and seize the day; get in and out before the hordes. You'll waste less time in lines and have fewer frustrating tourists ruining your snaps with their bumbags and screaming children. Failing waking up at the crack of dawn (we all know it's hard on holiday), aim for lunchtime, when some of the crowd will disappear for a bite to eat. Make sure you have your lunch well before or after, though; restaurants near attractions are notorious for tripling the price for half the quality.

If you're strapped for cash, have a look at what free activities are on offer in the area. You can find some great museums that are free of charge, or my personal favourite, amazing walking tours with an option to make a small donation at the end. These can range from street art to history to food crawls and are a great way to while away an afternoon spending next to no money and meeting a few friendly people along the way.

I like to zip around the main "must do" sights of the city first, and then I always plan for at least an extra couple of days in each place. Those unplanned days I love to spend getting purposefully lost, walking for hours and absorbing sights and sounds. I often find somewhere to sit, whether it be a café or park, and watch the world go by or read a book. This breathing space in each place lets you really get a feel for where you are instead of just rushing around manically ticking things off a bucket list.

Moving On

There are no hard-and-fast rules about what you should be enjoying. Hopefully, you've left your schedule pretty flexible, and if you're loving a city, stay an extra few days; if something's not up your street, move on. Moving continually can become exhausting, and I've often scheduled mini rest stops where I stay still on purpose – a juice detox in Thailand, a week of surfing lessons in Peru. There seems to be a constant pressure to race ahead to the next new experience, but if you're getting a bit jaded or templed-out, give yourself a break, book into a resort and read and relax if that's what you feel like doing.

Make your own rules! Plus spending more time in fewer places means spending less, reducing transport costs and stretching out your budget. Having to pack and unpack, and deal with endless airports, bus terminals, border crossings and visa issues, can get you down, so slow down and take more in. That way, you won't suffer from burnout, and you'll really get a feel for a place and learn about the cheap places to eat and cheap things to do.

Food

I tend to eat a lot of local food; it's easy on the purse strings and gives you a great insight into local culture.

Take the plunge and sample some street food. Many people shy away from it because of hygiene concerns, but I can honestly say that I've eaten bucketloads of street food from all over the world and the only two times I've had terrible food poisoning were both from fancy(ish) restaurants. Some of it might be hit and miss, but it's so cheap you can try a little of everything and be sure you're not missing out. The same thing goes for food markets. They are a great way to feel like you've had a night out while spending next to nothing. Wander around the stalls and see what takes your fancy. I once got served maggots in my bowl of noodles in the depths of Chinatown, Kuala Lumpur, but you just have to laugh and move on to the next vendor!

When you're away from your home culture, you have to redefine your "normal" food. If you're travelling Asia, you'll suddenly find much more rice and noodles in your diet; same with lobster in Cuba or curries in India. Just go with it as long as it suits your tummy! I love diving into the weird and wonderful foods you can find abroad, although I must say eating a guinea pig in Peru (it's their national food) really pushed my boundaries, as did eating a live scorpion in Laos.

After a few weeks away, constantly translating menus, having the same local flavours every day, it's normal to start craving things you miss from home. I never deny myself, and if I fancy some fast food, a fancy meal or a pizza, I go for it. Travelling is about making yourself happy, and as long as you are diving into local culture too, there's nothing wrong with a bit of home comfort now and again.

Cultural Submersion

Sometimes, when I'm travelling, I get bored with meeting travellers. I crave a bit more of an authentic experience than the usual trail and end up throwing myself in the deep end, happily, on purpose. A perfect way to do this is to get out of town. Out in the countryside, you can get a glimpse of what real life is like, away from tour groups, crime and locals trying to make a quick buck. You'll find the people friendlier and life cheaper. Sure, this offers more travel challenges; there will probably be little English uttered, and no taxis or cellular data, but that's all part of the fun. A smile and some hand gestures go a long way, I've found. Over the years, I have been lucky enough to volunteer at an ashram in southern India, stay in an orphanage in Venezuela and live in a homestay in Laos. These experiences stand out in my scrapbook of memories more than various nights out or cool hostels. None of them was booked, just stumbled upon by spending real time in places and interreacting with locals.

This is obviously a little easier if you can speak at least a token amount of the local language, especially if it's one like Spanish you can try and get your head around. But even in Asia where it's trickier, everyone has time to grasp a few basic words that will go a long way in the culture you are visiting.

Adventures just seem to appear in front of you when you put yourself out there. I was on a dive boat for the day once in Cozumel, Mexico, and got chatting with one of the other guests. He invited my travel bud and me over for a drink at his place after the dive, and we accepted – a margarita sounded really good to our salty taste buds. Turns out he was a multi-millionaire, and we spent the day at his huge mansion, drinking cocktails, playing in the infinity pool, meeting his family and eating some of the best Mexican food I'd ever tasted. Our hostel looked pretty measly that night in comparison, I can tell you. But if you don't make an effort to chat to others, you might be missing out!

Stuck in a Rut

It's quite easy, when you're long-term travelling, to get stuck in a negative routine of partying, especially if you've clicked in with a nice group that's mostly about doing that. While it's great fun for a while, you can easily find yourself going from town to town and really experiencing only the various nightclubs. Some destinations lend themselves to this more than others, and it's fine to have weeks that are boozier than others. While I'm all up for sampling what the local bar scene has to offer, keep checking in with yourself to ensure it's not all you're doing. You'll regret it when you return home if the only memories you have are those of hangovers and Jagerbombs. If you get stuck with a group of booze hounds, veer away from them for a few days and arrange to meet up along the way. On travel days or when you find yourself alone, give yourself a day off the sauce to let your body (and probably your mind) recover. It's easy to get into a bit of a drinking routine on the road, and although it's fun, it can get boring over time too, and it's not the healthiest.

Romance on the Road

When we are in the world's most beautiful places, with a cocktail in our hand, freedom pumping through our veins and a world of possibility at our feet, it's easy to get a little caught up in the moment. It's natural, especially after a few sundowners, to meet a like-minded fellow traveller and for romance to start to blossom. Passion on the road can be a whirlwind, with no rules or judgements; you are on holiday, after all.

While I'm all for getting caught up in someone every once in a while, just make sure you look after yourself. There have been plenty of stories of travellers taking someone home and waking up to everything stolen, or to an angry Thai girl demanding money. Keep your bag or wallet on your brain when someone is flirting outrageously with you at the bar; a little sleight of hand could result in not just your ego feeling hurt when they strut off.

Have your fun, do as you please, but always, always, always use protection. Some travellers seem on a mission to spread various venereal diseases amongst the backpacking community. And don't let yourself get dragged into anything dirty.

CHAPTER 6

STAYING SANE

Making Friends

Being alone when you're travelling really is a choice. Doing some research into social hostels is most of the effort. Many have weekly events or common areas you can hang out in, and most people staying there are in the same position as you. Most people love to chat to new people and share tips and a drink or three. Be proactive and start conversations, look approachable and don't hide behind your book or phone. A friendly smile is normally enough to spark up a conversation, and it usually flows easily.

At the end of the day, you already have so much common ground with those you meet. You're both open-minded enough to explore the world and can compare other places you've been or would like to go. The sheer breadth of different nationalities, occupations and life stories of the people one encounters is staggering and, for me, is one of the best parts of travelling. Remember, no one is going to come and knock on your door and invite you out; you have to throw yourself into the social mix and go with the flow. It doesn't really matter if the bar that people are going to isn't actually one that you would choose or if a certain restaurant doesn't tickle your fancy. Try and let the easy-going traveller in you come through; forming bonds and creating memories is so much more rewarding.

Having said that, don't be pressured into situations you feel uncomfortable with. If you don't want to go clubbing that night, then don't. If you meet people who are a little more into their illegal substances than you'd like, then distance yourself if you feel more comfortable. Design your own environment, and the right people will come to you. Also, be wary of being dragged into situations where a social group is a little more loaded than you. Breaking your budget every now and again is fine; doubling it every day for weeks to keep up is not. Be honest with your new friends, and they will be understanding. After all, you are all in the same boat!

Be patient and know that it takes time to feel comfortable in a new, unfamiliar environment. You can discover who you really are without the preconceptions of who you were at home. It really is a time to experiment, with no lasting judgements. If you feel yourself starting to panic or get overwhelmed, give yourself space to have some time out. Do something "normal" that you used to do at home to give you a tangibly ordinary experience – think go to the cinema, wander round a mall or go to the park. Just because you're travelling, it doesn't mean you can't do these things. Just make yourself happy in your new surroundings. Take a deep breath and then throw yourself back into it.

There can also be trust issues with meeting other travellers. While it is normally a positive experience, always be a little bit wary. There are stories of people choosing to room with someone and waking up with some of their things missing, or lending money to someone they've just met and then their new pal suddenly disappearing. Many travellers run out of money on their trip, and desperation can cause people to do some hurtful and horrible things. Just remember, at the end of the day, the only person responsible for you and your stuff is you.

Being Alone

Travelling alone is probably completely different from anything you have ever done before. No structure or support system, dealing with culture shock, not having a set schedule or routine – it can be overwhelming. Then there is the loneliness. This is a real fear and sometimes a real problem on the road, but I can honestly say the only times I've ever really felt lonely when I've been travelling have been when it was self-inflicted: when I've booked myself into a honeymooner-infested fancy hotel for a couple of nights, when I've taken off into the middle of the countryside and no one speaks my language, or when I've just gone through an antisocial few days (we all have them) and haven't made an effort with the people in my hostel.

It certainly takes some getting used to. With no one to consider, whole stretches of time to fill and no one to rely on, the loneliness and contrast from your life back home can be deafening. It is a skill to learn to love your own company. Learn it on the road, and it can pay you back ten times over for the rest of your life. Of course, being by yourself can present some practical challenges. Going to the toilet at a train station can lead to an awfully squashed stall when there's no one to watch your bag, and taking photos can be difficult, but screw it, buy a selfie stick if you must or ask a stranger. You will survive!

There is a beauty in the lack of compromise of being alone, doing what you want when you want, whether that's waking up at 2pm or going ice climbing. Travelling with a buddy can get claustrophobic, and even the best of friends tend to fall out sometimes when backpacking. The sheer number of couples who break up once they are around each other 24/7 is staggering.

You can decide your own schedule and do exactly as you please. I love having time with my thoughts and being free to wander and absorb without pressure from anybody, being able to dip in and out of social circles and find whatever works for me on any given day. Being alone doesn't have to be lonely, but there is a social stigma attached to being alone and a judgement that we often put on ourselves. Relish this moment of freedom and learn to embrace it.

One area that many people struggle with while travelling alone for the first time is the evening. It's one thing to go sightseeing or grab lunch by yourself, but how do you fill a whole night? In fact, there are lots of social activities you can do without feeling like a loner. How about visiting a night market where you can wander about and blend into the crowds? There are often guided nightlife tours in big cities that will take you bar hopping, and you are guaranteed to meet other people. Book tickets to a show or standing tickets to a gig. Once the music starts, you won't stand out and can enjoy yourself and dance the night away. Failing that, head to your nearest expat bar or Irish pub. While the décor and food selection might leave something to be desired, you'll find friendly people from back home; wherever you are in the world, sometimes you just miss hearing a familiar accent.

Another issue that people stumble over is eating, especially dinner. While grabbing lunch on the go is fine, when it comes to a sit-down meal, many people hate eating alone. This is definitely something that gets easier with time. It can take a little getting used to, not because it's difficult, but just because it's not something we do at home, and it goes against our ingrained social training. Honestly, at this point, it doesn't bother me in the slightest, and the more you travel, the less you care what people think. I take a good book or use the time to call home while I wait for my food and enjoy the occasion.

If you do feel awkward, though, there are a few tricks you can use to ease yourself into solo dining. Firstly, you can ask to be seated at the bar. It's a lot less exposed than a table for two (for one), and you can strike up a conversation with the barman or whoever's next to you. Café or casual dining can feel less strange than a fancy restaurant and is a good option for sitting down to write a journal entry while you wait. Just check to make sure they have Wi-Fi before you make yourself comfy! You can always find some dinner companions if you want to. Try eatwith.com or voulezvousdiner.com for some original social options for solo diners in a new city, combining tasty food, cultural immersion and interesting new friends. It's a great way to throw yourself into a destination.

If restaurant dining really isn't for you, why not try a cooking class with a meal at the end of it or grabbing something to go from a food truck or street food vendor. There are so many options, and you'll probably save money in the process!

Homesickness

Homesickness can be a very real and sometimes debilitating problem. Missing friends, family, significant others, colleagues and routines from home can feel crushing at times, to the point where you're just not enjoying the places you've worked so hard to experience. It's hard to be away from everything you know, and some people definitely feel this more keenly than others.

Take time to recognise your feelings. It's better to have some quiet time and a good think to realise what's getting you down, rather than just pretending that it's all ok. Talk to other travellers about it and get a sense of proportion. You are not away forever: you will be back at home in your normal routine in however many weeks or months and, I bet, wishing like hell you were still drifting about in the sunshine. Recognise that the feelings associated with being so far away are completely normal, but just because you miss something or someone, it doesn't mean you can't enjoy the present.

Try and stay in touch with your home life. Phone or message friends; video call if you can. It will offer you reassurance that they are missing you as much as you are missing them. I often find that when I'm feeling a little too far from home, a little chat about daily life – someone's grocery shopping, dad telling me what the neighbours are up to, or your friend's boss giving them grief is normally enough to make me feel very lucky to be away from life's mundane but necessary evils. Staying in touch is important as it will make your transition back into life at home so much easier if you haven't just dropped off the face of the planet. Show an interest in people's lives at home, and don't only talk about all the fun you're having.

There is a fine balance with staying in touch, and if you find yourself talking with loved ones for hours each day, then maybe it's time to live in the moment a little more. Distract yourself by getting out there and having fun and not wasting time wishing you were somewhere else.

Make sure your phone is loaded up with photos of your nearest and dearest. A quick flick through on a long bus ride can bring a smile to your face when you feel so very far away. Feelings of homesickness have to be recognised, checked and put in perspective before they become a constant hum. Yes, you miss your creature comforts, your partner or bestie, but you chose to leave them, and they will still be there when you get back. Take a deep breath and plan an amazing homecoming party for your return. You'll have so much to catch up on.

Staying in Touch

There are so many ways to stay connected with home when you're away. When I first went travelling, you had to make time to go to an internet café every few days to send long email updates about what you'd been up to or pay extortionate amounts to use the landline.

Now the advent of smartphones and the explosion of the internet has made life much easier. From sharing your stunning photos on Instagram to sending quick updates on Whatsapp, Skype calls home to mum and dad, and jealousy-inducing Facebook status updates, there is a huge variety of ways to keep in contact.

Making the effort to send a quick message, letting people know you're safe, sharing the highs and the lows, can make you feel much more secure and lets others at home share along in your experience. Why not start a travel blog for an easy way to let the masses know about your adventures? When you're home, it's very rewarding to read back through it.

It's easy to focus on yourself when you're away, but when you call, be sensitive to the fact that they are not island hopping or bungee jumping but are dealing with traffic jams, coping with a heavy work schedule and doing the laundry. No one likes a travel bore. Remember that you will be back there living that life at some point, so ask questions, listen to the answers, and keep up with the updates on their lives; sharing is a two-way street.

CHAPTER 7

STAYING SAFE

Attitude

Safety is obviously a huge issue while you're travelling and one that is probably a big concern before you leave, especially when going it solo and, sadly, even more so for females. A certain amount of research can mean that you end up in the good areas of town, rather than the more dangerous ones, but at the end of the day, crime happens all over the world and comes in all kinds of unwanted shapes and surprises. I get it: it's cool to rock up somewhere new and be constantly amazed by new stuff because you haven't done any research and don't know what to expect. The thing is, though, arriving in a new country totally naïve or oblivious to the culture, religion, language and customs is just plain risky.

Your dad is not Liam Neeson, I presume? Don't worry, you will not be Taken. Unless he's been living some MI5-style double life you know nothing about, your dad does not have a particular set of skills wanted by any government, and I'd go so far as to guess he struggles to find the remote, let alone you. You'll be fine. But you do need to watch out for the day-to-day incidents that come part and parcel of travelling. There will always be risk, but do what you can to minimise it. Check in often with home and let someone know where you are. It takes two seconds to send a message with a hotel name, something that you will regret not doing should some disaster happen.

Staying off the radar makes a huge difference to your general safety on the road. It is definitely something that takes time to get used to, but just simple things like wearing clothes that blend in and leaving your flashy designer labels behind, along with anything particularly revealing, is, for us ladies, essential. The less you have with you, the less there is to steal, and I take nothing travelling that I can't bear to part with. Sitting in a taxi in Lima, Peru, in 2007, I had a slick-fingered local reach through the open window while I was sat at a traffic light and grab the sunglasses off my head. More fool him as they cost $5 from a street stall, but it goes to show, you can almost never switch off.

This applies equally to your technology. While it's easy to replicate phone-related behaviours from home when you're away, be aware that the phone you are holding may be worth six months' salary to the person who may snatch it. Be aware of when and how you use your technology. Duck into a café to check your Google Maps if you're somewhere a little dodgy, and don't keep your phone in your back pocket. Your phone is your lifeline when you're away, and you need to protect it! By all means, use it to take photos and enhance your travels, but just do so consciously, with an awareness of your surroundings.

Being low key is a skill that must be instilled in you; more than what you wear, it's an attitude. Not being the loudest or drunkest at the bar will mean that you will not become a target for enterprising locals. Try not to stand out or cause any offence; nudity and loutish behaviour, while sometimes fun, are not as readily accepted in most cultures you will visit and can mean unwanted attention from locals or police who are sick of western tourists treating their country as a giant dive bar.

Blend in. Act local, look local, be local… This is, of course, sometimes laughably impossible, but do what you can. If you decide to don the national dress, this can often work as a pretty good icebreaker. Blending in will help you be culturally sensitive, as well, and you will attract less attention. If you're visiting a country that dresses conservatively even in the worst heat, then suck it up, you need to respect the local customs and dress that way too. Wandering through the streets of Laos topless or in a bikini is disrespectful, and you will stand out like a sore thumb. Doing this in somewhere like India (Goa ain't India, folks!) is just plain stupid.

Exude an air of confidence while you're wandering around. Don't be the meek, nervous tourist that you might feel inside, shaking while you panic over a (probably upside down) map. Having confidence, even if it's a sham (you will build it up eventually) helps you to not stand out as a target. A smile and a little white lie ("I'm meeting friends") or wearing a cheap fake wedding ring can go a long way to keeping you safe. Give strong, firm answers to questions from locals. If they see hesitation or a flicker of doubt, they will pounce, and a strong but polite refusal to offers of tours or souvenirs is all you need. You ever notice it's the same people who get hounded time and time again by street sellers, massage girls and taxi drivers? Being overly nice won't get you far on the road, and in fact can cause you a lot of hassle. Don't promise to come back later or think about it. Just say no thank you – job done.

It's easy to become careless over time. When you start your travels, you are hyper-vigilant and pretty damn careful, but you gradually become accustomed to being on the road, and that level of personal security tends to drop and you become complacent. Try and stay focused, and know that if there have been no incidents, it's because it's working!

Accidents

I'm actually not going to tell you not to drink and drive because if you do drink and drive, you probably won't listen to me anyway. Protect yourself and protect your trip of a lifetime by wearing a helmet, especially when you have been drinking. I'm a good driver; I've driven in lots of crazy countries around the world. It doesn't matter how good you are; if you ride or drive everywhere, you will eventually have an accident. I've come off a motorbike three times. On two occasions, I was absolutely fine. On the only occasion when I wasn't wearing a helmet, I cut my face up and had to get nine stitches above my eye. Wear your helmet; it could save your life.

While I was working as a dive instructor in Koh Tao, Thailand, I had the privilege of meeting literally thousands of backpackers. I would say, as a conservative estimate, that one in five ends up in some sort of scooter accident. I'm not sure why people think they suddenly have the skills to drive a moped when they would never consider it at home. At best, you end up with a lovely exhaust burn on your inner ankle, a "Thailand tattoo". I did see the worst, and it happened on a quad bike. People think quad bikes are safer because they have four wheels, but they flip very easily, and people often end up with broken necks instead of grazes and sprained ankles. One horrible day stands out in my mind. One of my students I had been teaching for the past three days didn't show up for his course. This being a somewhat common occurrence due to the tempting nightlife on the island, I ventured up to his room to turf him out of bed. I was informed by his distraught friend that he had died the night before, after flipping a quad bike and breaking his neck. Traffic accidents are still the number one killer of backpackers. Be careful.

The number two cause of death for backpackers? Drowning. Every year, on every continent, some backpacker will get drunk or stoned out of their mind and then decide it's a fantastic idea to go swimming. I get it, and I've done it. Being in the sea while smashed is great fun, but you have to take some precautions. I don't go deep or swim off beaches that might have currents I don't know about. Be aware of the added risk when you are drunk and avoid swimming. When I was living in Thailand, I saw numerous day-glow-painted, unconscious twenty-somethings getting pulled up the beach from the incoming tide by their ankles. Don't be one of them.

Keeping yourself safe while travelling is largely using your common sense. When you're liquored up with a bunch of new mates, it's easy to be convinced to do something stupid – like climbing scaffolding, balancing five people on a scooter or swimming in a fast-moving river in the dark. I've found myself in all of those situations while travelling, and on those occasions, I've known that it was a bad idea. If you know it's a bad idea, don't do it – screw the peer pressure and just walk away.

Medical care abroad is often patchy and pay for play, especially on small islands. I once helped a friend I found on the side of the road after coming off his scooter. We got him to a clinic, and the nurses made me go to an ATM and withdraw cash before they'd even open the door.

Even the most careful traveller will get into the occasional scrape or three, and private hospital bills can really add up. Proper insurance that covers you for what you will actually be doing (scuba diving/skydiving/skiing) is not expensive and is an absolutely essential cost of travelling. If you can't afford insurance, you can't afford to go. Period.

Transport

Transport can be a tricky one. You often have to get separated from your bag, maybe need to sleep, and have to place your trust in whoever is transporting you. The level of comfort you opt for can often be predetermined by your budget, but you can still make sensible choices, even if you are shoestringing it.

Do your research before you book anything. When travelling through Bolivia, I was warned about the buses. (During the month I was travelling there, around 60 people died in bus accidents.) Bolivian roads can be very dangerous as most of them are still unpaved, and in the rainy season, landslides are common in the mountain regions. Furthermore, the bus drivers sometimes drink and drive or drive when overtired and cause accidents. In those countries, I decided to go for the more expensive tourist options. The buses were modern and less likely to break down, they had more security to protect their reputations, and on overnight buses, they mostly had two drivers. In the end, it cost only a few bucks more.

In Thailand, some bus companies are known for stowing a Thai child or two in the baggage compartment to rifle through your belongings and pilfer while you're sound asleep upstairs. Keep your valuables with you in your carry-on and keep your eyes on it at all times. If you need to sleep, use it as a pillow or keep your arms wrapped around it.

For local transport, know where you are going before you get in a taxi, and follow the ride on Google Maps to make sure you are heading in the right direction. Always haggle over a price before you get in, and have a definite destination in mind. Don't ask for "a mall" but have a Google first and choose the one you want. Otherwise, you'll find yourself two hours away with a smiling taxi driver who has just lined his pockets. If you do get a taxi to a remote destination, think about whether it's worth arranging a return fare. This can often cost more for their waiting time, but it's better than getting stranded. Always make sure your taxi is registered and the meter is running.

I have become very wary of tuk-tuks over time, especially in Thailand. They often refuse to take you anywhere other than the places where they get commission. I have been abandoned outside brothels on numerous occasions, and they generally overcharge by a long way. I'm not saying that trying to fit ten of you on the back of one on the way to a ping-pong show and persuading the driver to do wheelies isn't fun, but I feel lucky to have come away from that one not needing a hospital visit.

Party Safe

There is a party to be had in every country. It's hard not to get lured in with cheap local beer and, depending on the country, some pretty cheap drugs. Before you know it, the room is swaying and you probably should have stopped drinking two Changs ago. Alcohol, drugs and staying safe while travelling are not a reliable mix. Know your limits, when to stop and go home. If you are on a mission to get smashed, then do it with someone you trust. The new friends you just met at the bar probably aren't going to be reliable when you are wasted.

You can be well prepared and follow all the tips and recommendations, but sometimes your fellow travellers can get you into trouble with their behaviour. If you decide to travel with somebody, make sure you share the same travel philosophy in matters of safety. If you run into trouble, discuss the situation with your friend. If they keep acting stupid, you should split up. I was in a bar in Indonesia once when an old school friend thought it was hilarious to lean over and steal a bottle of rum from behind the bar. It was hilarious, until the tiny female bartender smashed him over the head with it and we ended our evening running away from the police and gracing the local emergency room for stitches.

Arrange a place and a time to meet your friends if you get lost. Always try to go out and go home as a group. When it gets dark, it also gets more dangerous in most places. If you are taking drugs or getting drunk, write the address of your hostel on your phone, or even better, take a business card from the hostel front desk. Trust me, there is nothing fun about wandering around late at night (or early in the morning) looking for your hostel when you have no idea where it is or even what it's called….

Beware the sudden appearance of beautiful strangers…or even average-looking strangers. The world is full of truly lovely people, but every now and again you meet someone who is just too damn nice. And sometimes these "too damn nice" people are looking to make money out of you somehow. They may simply try to sell you something. Or, they may rob you. Keep your wits about you, especially if you are drinking, and keep an eye on your stuff and your drink.

I once let a guy buy me a drink in a bar in Cuzco, Peru. I wasn't really interested in him, and it was my first drink of the night. I thought I was watching him the whole time, but it only takes the tiniest sleight of hand to slip something into a drink. Fast forward to my being found locked inside a toilet, unconscious, four hours later and the police driving me around, looking for my hostel from a business card they'd found in my handbag. I was lucky; I obviously had the sense to take myself away and lock myself up in safety, but it gave me a bad shock. Other than a day spent hugging a toilet bowl, I was unscathed, but I had a renewed sense of awareness of my surroundings and a decent dose of suspicion about new friends.

Be protective of information. No one needs to know if your parents have money or where you plan to be next. Be friendly and vague and wary if anyone is pressing too hard for any specifics about you.

In Koh Phangan, the island of full-moon parties and general debauchery, I would regularly witness young men limping, slightly charred and ashamed, to the various clinics around town. Turns out you could pay good money to limbo under a fire stick or jump rope with a burning skipping rope. Obvious drunk tourists think this is a fantastic idea and sign up immediately. Please think it through before joining in, those burns get awfully infected after a few days of sunshine, sand and sweat melting into them.

I was standing around watching a 'professional' fire show one fateful evening with two Thai guys throwing a ball of fire to one another in various loop-the-loops and other such impressive formations. It was pretty remarkable and there was a fairly large crowd watching them, the crowd seemed less impressed however when one of the guys missed a catch and sent a burning ball of flames into a poor Dutch girl's face. Stand back from fire shows people.

Your Stuff

Your backpack is your house, your lifeline and your key to comfort on the road; treat it as such. Never leave it or trust random strangers to watch it for a period of time. If you have a few hours to waste before a train or bus, check out local left-luggage facilities which allow you to explore worry free.

Split up your bank cards and emergency cash into a few separate places. That way, if something does go missing, you have a back-up ready to go. If you are in a particularly dangerous area, try and use ATMs inside banks or malls rather than on the street and keep a dummy wallet available to give away in a worst-case scenario. Having been mugged at gunpoint at an ATM in Nicaragua, I can safely say that it is not fun, and it left me very shaken up. Take some time to find a proper bank ATM or team up with a traveller that you really trust. Someone is much less likely to approach the pair of you if one is playing lookout.

If your hotel or hostel has a safe, use it! Hotels often won't accept any liability for items left around in your room, and unfortunately, your passport or phone can represent a year's worth of wages for local staff and can prove all too tempting. While on the beach, keep your money and phone on you in a dry bag when swimming; sometimes people are literally waiting for you to take a dip to swipe something of value, and there's nothing like a stolen wallet to ruin your glow.

Be even more careful at large tourist attractions. Small children or other distractions are often used to get your attention while your pockets are picked. Keep your valuables carefully stashed away and your wits about you to avoid trouble.

Sexual Harassment

Unfortunately, even in this day and age, we single ladies often get dealt the brunt of traveller harassment, especially in certain developing countries. I certainly felt this much more keenly when travelling through India and certain Arab countries. In these kinds of places, I make a special effort to not put myself in danger. I will always stay in nice hotels, get taxis everywhere and try to never walk alone after dark or on lonely streets. It's a sad state of affairs but a very real one when it happens to you. I usually make sure I'm wearing baggy, hi-cut pants and t-shirts and no makeup as it seems to lessen the effect. I've learnt to sit in the back seat of a taxi, on the opposite side to the driver, after a certain incident in Cairo where one got awfully handsy.

Be extremely firm with any unwanted advances, as a slight hesitation can be taken as encouragement, and read up on the places you go beforehand to get the lie of the land. I was backpacking through Morocco, and Marrakesh was absolutely fine. Off the beaten track, however, I found people spitting in my face at the sight of my blonde hair. I was travelling during Ramadan, and turns out this increases the antagonism towards western women; a little research would have made me alter my travel dates.

I once checked into a hotel in Egypt and had the very unpleasant experience of a staff member trying to get into my room during the night. Fortunately, I had the chain on the door, and when I shouted, he ran off. I hate to think what would have happened otherwise. Once I'd left the hotel, I had repeated phone calls and emails from someone I assume was the same staff member, who had stolen my contact information from the front desk! When I called and informed the management, this immediately stopped, and I was offered a free stay in exchange for my inconvenience. Needless to say, I didn't take them up on it.

Harassment and assault are situations that female

travellers encounter and must learn to deal with. If you're in an area where harassment is common, even travelling with one other person helps. If you're travelling solo, be prepared to answer questions about your fake (or real) boyfriend, and determine how you would handle some of these situations. Read up on sexual harassment when you travel, as the situations vary, and it happens to different degrees depending on where you're headed.

If you're a male reader, be aware and considerate of solo female travellers in countries where harassment is common. Even sitting next to one of us on public transport or walking alongside us helps to decrease the comments or assaults.

Police

This can be a bit of a contentious issue, obviously depending on the kind of country you are travelling to. In the western world, we are brought up with intrinsic trust in the police, and it can take some time to get your head around the fact that they are not always on your side.

While I would always recommend going to or phoning the police if you are in imminent danger, or if your things have been stolen and you need a report for insurance, I hesitate to get involved with them much more than that.

While I was living in Thailand, the police were known to be outrageously corrupt. Plain-clothes "police officers" were prevalent at full moon parties, offering tourists drugs and then extorting bribes from them when they revealed a (maybe fake, who knows) badge. In Peru, I was arrested and actually put in handcuffs because there was one too many of us in the back of a taxi. Again, a few tattered notes quickly got my wrists free again.

In Columbia, I got into an unfortunate situation with the police on two occasions within a month, in disturbingly similar circumstances. Both times, I was "randomly" searched, roughly pushed up against a wall and quite intimately patted down. Unsurprisingly, in both instances, they "found" a little bag of cocaine, which had most definitely not been in my pocket two minutes before. I was forced to pay $50 on the first occasion and $100 on the next, under threat of being arrested if I did not cough up. Now to me, the thought of rotting in a Colombian jail is not a happy one, so I just paid it, but the fact that this goes on, especially with such regularity, is quite disturbing.

It's illegal to offer a bribe to police officers. Plus, if you take part in bribery, you're perpetuating the cycle and probably driving up the price. But being subtle in the phrasing of the bribe goes a long way. Instead of calling it a bribe, people ask if there's a "special fee" they can pay the official to speed up the process, or if they can pay the fine "on-the-spot", or if they can "help" the official in some way.

One of favourite police-related situations (of which there seem to be many) happened whilst I was living in Honduras. I was somewhat inebriated after consuming one or twenty gin and tonics at a bar in town, and when it was time to go home, it suddenly seemed like very far away. A lovely couple who are very dear friends of mine offered to drive me on their motorbike, they're designed for 3 people right? It was all going so well until we got a sudden police check point, we obviously got stopped and there were flashes of large semi-automatic weapons and lots of Spanish shouting. After we stood for a while looking suitably sheepish, I decided with gin-elevated confidence to approach the police officer in question, give him a gentle arm stroke, bat my eyelashes and use my best Spanish to breathily say "lo siento". To our collective astonishment it worked and I went to start the long walk home afoot, until the officer motioned for me to reboard the bike and continue our perilous journey. I wouldn't exactly recommend this method (both as forms of transport and police relations go) but never underestimate your power girls!

Although illegal, bribery is common, and the locals admit they rationalize it by thinking of it as a way to honour and respect the status of the person who's helping their day go more smoothly. Need a stamp in your passport, but it's going to take a couple of days? You'll be amazed at the time-travel properties of 100 baht, or so I'm told.

There is little to be done about these unfortunate goings on; just use your smarts and try and get out of any sticky situations. I would much rather pay a bribe than be arrested. To make any dealings with foreign police a little smoother, follow these tips:

- Be courteous and act reasonably at all times.
- Don't raise your voice, or make demands and threats.
- If you're in the wrong, expect little mercy and be prepared to pay an on-the-spot fine.
- If you're in a dispute with a local, it's likely the police will side with the local, even if you're not at fault. Just accept this.
- Don't smile or talk to a police officer unless he talks to you first.

- Don't be a dumb tourist and draw attention to yourself by being drunk or loud.

- Don't make a false statement to police, even for an insurance claim. It's illegal.

Worst Case Scenario

Trust your gut, it's intelligent. Sometimes there is nothing wrong about trusting your instincts when booking a tour or a bus ride or making a decision about the next travel destination. If something feels wrong, it maybe is wrong – if in doubt: trust your instincts!

Don't play the hero. If you run into a situation where you get mugged, you should act wisely and follow the instructions. In those situations, resistance often leads to more violence – it is much better to give away your camera than your health.

If you get physically attacked by someone, fight back, hard. Your life could depend on it. Once you have them down, run somewhere public and get the heck out of Dodge. If you're touched inappropriately or feel threatened in public, make a scene and draw attention. Someone will always come to help or stand up for you; this is commonplace in many cultures such as India and the Middle East. If you have to fight, go for the throat and eyes.

Recovery

I was living in Venezuela, on my own, when I was 18 years old. A questionable decision at best. One day, I was on a local bus, on the 15-minute journey back to my hostel from the beach, when five guys with guns stood up from their seats. One held up the driver, and the others went through the bus collecting money from people. They saw me, an obvious westerner, and brought me out to the front of the crowd. I obviously gave them any money I had (about $10) and my bag, which contained a book and some sunglasses. They seemed displeased with their gains, having obviously presumed I was a cash cow. They proceeded to beat me up pretty badly over the next two hours, screaming at me in Spanish while I listened to the sound of my ribs crunching and the taste of blood filled my mouth. After what seemed like eternity, they threw me off the moving bus onto the road and left me for dead. I have no memory of the next few hours, but I've been told I was found on my hostel steps unconscious. Apparently, some kind-hearted stranger must have driven me back and dumped me there. My memory restarts some time that evening. I had been checked out by a doctor who had decided it was superficial damage, a few sprains strapped up from the fall and broken ribs which they could do nothing about. I was lying in the bed of the owner of the hostel, the most comfortable place for me.

The only fortunate thing about the situation was that I was due to fly home two days later, anyway. So I called my dad to warn him about the new shape of my face, booked special assistance from the airline to help me with my bags, and started the 30-hour journey home through taxis, a ferry and three flights to Heathrow. I had never been so excited to see my parents until I saw the fear reflected in their faces due to the state of mine.

I was very shaken up for a while, extremely jumpy, and I still hate guns to this day, but I had a choice to make. I had an eight-week trip around Thailand and Cambodia booked in a month's time. Should I cancel it? It was a hard decision, but I went for it, and I am so happy I did.

Sometimes when you travel, bad stuff happens, but it's how you deal with it that counts. The important lesson I learnt was that I no longer wanted to travel to such dangerous places and that there were enough other countries in the world that didn't put me at such a high risk. I still make choices with that in mind, now. Learn what you can from the bad times, and adjust your travel style or keep a more watchful eye in future. Unfortunately, no matter how much we read and prepare before we travel, sometimes lessons have to be learnt the hard way. Don't let it send you home or put you off. Talk about it with others, take some time to process and recover, and then smash on.

CHAPTER 8

STAYING HEALTHY

Fitness

Staying healthy while you're away can be a challenge. Away from any set routine or exercise, a little more temptation in your way in terms of local beer and local girls, and a diet of snacks and constant meals out can take its toll, fast.

When most people think of exercise, they usually think of people torturing themselves in a gym with weight machines and running on treadmills like a hamster for hours at a time. Besides, when you're travelling, the LAST thing you want to be thinking about is being cooped up in a gym when you should be out exploring your new surroundings.

We only get one chance on this planet, and we only have one body to do it in, so we should probably take care of ourselves. Luckily, if we can do some basic things and put a few key systems in place while travelling (and when we're not travelling), we'll be ready to do whatever, wherever, whenever. To start (and hopefully this goes without saying), doing things like riding your bike, hiking and going for walking tours is a fantastic start to building a healthy body. It's exercise that doesn't really feel like exercise because you're also exploring new locations. Find a workout you can have saved on your phone that you can do in any park, hotel room or playground. Interval training is a great way to get your heart rate up fast and can burn fat fast without burning up your sightseeing time! If you only have five minutes here and there, that's fine. Do squats when you can. Crank out a few pull-ups when you find something to hang from while on your hike, or bust out a plank in an epic location because why the hell not.

Exercise doesn't need to consume your life, either. It can be as simple as making an effort to sign up for a walking tour, opting to ride a bike through a city and getting lost on purpose, or hiking on small trips to prepare yourself for bigger trips. You can also mix in some activities that don't feel like exercise but are, like Tango lessons in Argentina, a yoga week in Bali or Muay Thai boxing in Thailand.

Regardless of your level of fitness, there are fun activities native to the countries you're visiting that can make for a great way to meet new people, train in an activity that is new to you and get your heart racing! I like to think of them as missions or quests to complete in addition to just seeing the sights, but that's just the nerd in me.

Diet

Diet is 80% of the battle! Nobody wants to hear this while travelling, but how you eat will account for 80–90 per cent of how you look and feel. Seriously! You can't outrun a bad diet, and you can't out-train one, either. What we're trying to avoid is the depression and crash dieting that follows a trip full of overeating abroad.

This is something I struggled with when I began travelling until I made a commitment to myself to start eating better, which required me to start spending more money on food (to get protein, vegetables, etc.). I either saved up more money before I went on my trip (a few bucks can mean a great meal in many countries!) or saved it elsewhere (by spending fewer nights out drinking). It requires a bit of discipline, but if you're committed to staying healthy and not wrecking your body (and waistline!) while travelling, it requires you to make some changes.

What we're aiming for is food that keeps us satiated and on target, i.e., mostly vegetables, some form of protein (be it from animal sources or legumes) and then some fruits and/or nuts – occasionally a bit of rice or potatoes and minimal bread or pasta or liquid calories.

You don't need to eat just broccoli and chicken when travelling and ignore anything that tastes good. Instead, try to make 80% of your meals healthy and then eat whatever you want the other few meals. Your body won't balloon up after one bad meal, but if you let one bad meal become a month of eating poorly, it will cause problems.

So find balance: if you are going to eat a big, unhealthy dinner, eat a small breakfast and lunch. If you've just had a massive breakfast, skip lunch – it evens out at the end of the day. Skipping a meal can be called intermittent fasting and can be really beneficial, actually!

I also implement the "never two in a row" rule. I never eat two bad meals in a row. If I'm in a location known for something unhealthy and delicious, I make sure the meals before and after are really healthy, so one bad meal doesn't become a habit.

Alcohol

Here's something you already know: drinking alcohol isn't exactly healthy for you. But then again, neither is staying up too late, not spending enough time in the sunlight, spending too much time in the sunlight, playing video games for too long, eating unhealthy foods, etc.

And yet we all do lots of these things; we have to make trade-offs while we live our lives and have some fun. If you decide that you want to drink, good for you. If you decide that you don't want to drink, that's fine too. You know yourself best; be smart.

Wine and liquor (sipped slowly) without mixers are the "healthiest" options. Light beers and good beers are next best, in moderation. Sugary mixed drinks or energy drink-and-alcohol combos (I see you, Thailand!) are terrible for you. Sugar is literally the devil. Now, calories from drinks can really add up, as can the crappy food you consume when you're drunk… so try to party with purpose. Wine, beer, liquor. Know yourself and be smart about it.

Hygiene

Hygiene can certainly be an issue while travelling, and it helps if you can slightly lower your expectations before you go. You will not find the same standards abroad that you will in western countries – period. You might see the occasional rat or have geckos in your room, and using more than a few questionable toilet facilities is a certainty. Get used to it! Do what you can to protect yourself, of course. Keeping some hygiene wipes available for the times when there's no toilet paper to be found can be helpful, as can a little bottle of hand sanitizer if you feel so inclined. Squat toilets are part and parcel of travelling in many countries, so the best thing to do is grin and bear it – just think of it as an excellent thigh workout!

Never forget where you are. One morning, I awoke in Vietnam to find I had made the brilliant decision the night before to get my tragus (the middle bit of my ear) pierced. This was all well and good until it got really infected, making me pretty miserable. I have since got two tattoos abroad but was sober enough to fully check out the facility and needles first, and I looked after the area afterwards.

Sleep

It sounds obvious, but sleep is a huge factor in staying healthy and enjoying yourself. In long-term travelling, make sure you aren't burning the candle at both ends. Partying and experiencing cities can leave little time in the middle for your body to rest and rejuvenate, so if you've been out a few nights in a row, try an early night once in a while to catch up.

Try and grab naps while on transport and avoid jet lag

by quickly forcing yourself into the sleep hours of your newly adopted region. I always do this on the plane by setting my watch to my destination's time as soon as I'm on board and sticking to those general sleeping hours. Your body will thank you for it when you get there. And skip the wine on the plane. There's nothing worse than landing with a hangover.

Sleep quality is a factor, too. The fact is a night on a bus or naps on the beach are not high-quality sleep. Make sure you have a nice, restful environment where you can grab some first-rate rest. At least once in a while, try and opt for a private room where you can have a beautiful few hours of undisturbed snoozing.

Try and schedule rest stops into your travelling. If I know I'm heading somewhere that's heavy on the party scene, I'll pick somewhere a bit quieter for after, have a few days reading a book on the beach and let my body recover. If you do nothing but party for months on end, you will find your health, and bank balance, severely depleted.

Illness

Let's face it, there's nothing worse than getting ill while you're away from home. You crave creature comforts, your duvet, and can suddenly seem very, very far away from home.

No matter how invincible we feel when we're out exploring the wild, sometimes our body can only handle so much, and it reacts like a human body normally would. Add to this the weird and wonderful locations we visit, different hygiene standards and questionable water purity, and it can be a recipe for disaster. Make sure you research the area you are travelling to and have the required malaria meds or other vaccinations, and make sure you actually take them!

I was in Baños, Ecuador. I'd had a wonderful time horseback riding up the volcano and canyoning through waterfalls. It was time to move on, and I boarded the bus for the ten-hour ride to my next destination. About an hour into the journey, I felt the familiar rumble-slosh of my stomach, and fear gripped me. I guzzled Imodium, but it was no use. I spent the next nine hours trapped in hell. With no towns before the final destination for me to duck out to, I only had one choice: to stay on the bus ride from hell, watching the other passengers quietly remove themselves from my vicinity and cram themselves into the back of the bus, leaving me with my sick bags and changes of clothes. When we arrived, I got a taxi to a pharmacy, stocked up on Gatorade, rehydration sachets and crackers and barricaded myself in a hotel room for two days. Not my finest hour. Another time in

Thailand, I ended up on a drip from e-coli poisoning, a lovely way to enjoy Koh Samui.

These things happen when you're travelling, but the key is to try and minimise the likelihood of catching something and to get the right help when you do. Know when you can deal with it yourself and when it's gone too far and you need medical help.

Be careful of local water. Just because the locals drink it doesn't mean we can, with the same going for ice. If you do get ill, make sure you rest and give yourself time to recover. I remember being determined to have a great night out after recovering from a dicky tummy in the Gili islands in Indonesia; after all, it was New Year's Eve. I took a bunch of medicine that pepped me up, got all dressed up and felt half normal, got to a bar and drank a Long Island Iced Tea, and threw it up in a bush ten minutes later. Sometimes it's better not to push it.

Being ill is miserable at the best of times and even worse when you're away from home. The best you can do is get into some comfy accommodation and buckle down with a (hopefully English) movie channel.

If you have more than a cold or a spot of diarrhoea, get yourself to a doctor. If you need medicine, it's better to get it sooner rather than later and give yourself time to recover. Make sure you contact your insurance company; they'll point you in the right direction to a facility that's covered by your policy, and keep your receipts to claim.

If you are sick in countries where the health system is marginal at best, you are in for a bumpy ride. Some countries can barely sustain a health program for their own people, let alone the needs of visitors. For dangerous, poor and unstable areas, the more preventative measures you can take the better because once you are in the thick of it, it can be very hard to negotiate a good doctor. This is where your travel insurance company can be of great assistance; opt for private healthcare options if you can.

Altitude sickness is real and can be very dangerous. If you're planning on going hiking (or even hanging out) at altitude, make sure you know the signs and symptoms and be prepared to drop your altitude back down if you start to feel them. Who gets affected is very random, but the effects can be debilitating. Take it seriously and you'll be golden!

It might sound obvious, but make sure you bring (and actually use) sunscreen. Not only are tan lines not particularly attractive, but sun stoke is horrible and can lead to days of your trip stuck inside in pain or even a hospital visit in extreme cases. The sun is so much stronger than what you're probably used to at home, so try not to spend too much time catching rays, stay sun safe and unwrinkly.

Finally, it's better to be safe than sorry. Many travellers get a bout of illness and simply brush it off as lethargy, booking into a luxury suite to sleep it off. But are you a doctor? The symptoms of Dengue Fever are like mild flu, if any appear at all, and the effects of that illness can be devastating. So, if you get sick, do your best to get it checked out right away.

CHAPTER 9

MONEY

Sticking to a Budget

Sticking to a budget while you're away is no easy thing. There are so many opportunities to take amazing tours, do awesome activities and, let's face it, party. These are life-changing, perspective-altering things that should definitely be indulged in but can also run you into trouble when you get home.

It's important to be aware of what you're spending and what you've got left. You don't want to come home after two weeks because you've blown all your money on five-star hotels, helicopter rides and champagne. The thousands you have in your bank account at the start of the trip might seem like a lot when you're setting out, but after a few months on the road, you'll be kicking yourself if you've spent too much early on.

Some people go as far as keeping a record of everything they spend. While that might seem a bit excessive, if you use Revolut, as I recommended earlier on, the app has an amazing analysis tool. You can set a monthly budget, and it will send you notifications of how much you have left to spend for the day or month, as well as allocate your spending so you can see where your cash is going. You can set a regular payment to the card from your bank account, thus making sure you're not accidentally going over your limit.

Sometimes, sticking to a budget might mean eating street food instead of at a restaurant or missing out on a nightclub. But believe me, that last month before your flight home can be pretty miserable if you haven't rationed your funds properly. I have seen many a backpacker have to fly home early or literally beg food off other people in the hostel. Make sure you don't get into that situation by making a plan and sticking to it. When I travelled to Las Vegas, I literally ate subway for 90% of my meals because it meant that I could afford a helicopter flight over the Grand Canyon. It's all about priorities.

It's great to keep on top of your money, but make sure you keep some extra money aside for treats. You don't want to miss out on a once-in-a-lifetime opportunity to bungee-jump with dolphins because you've spent all your budget for that week. Whatever you do, keep a good chunk of money aside for unexpected problems. However much you plan, they always seem to crop up somewhere along the line. If you're lucky and don't need it, you'll have the luxury of arriving home to a bank account that's not completely empty.

Be very careful about putting things on credit cards while you're away. It might seem like a great idea at the time, but the only thing worse than getting back from travelling is getting back from travelling with a large credit card bill and no job to pay it off. I carry a credit card, but it's for real emergencies, not cocktails.

Take time once a month to reassess your budget. Is it going to plan? Are you going to have to readjust your travel lifestyle? These checkpoints are important, and a budget–per-day rejig might be needed to stretch your cash out over your remaining time. Be honest with yourself, and don't hide from your dwindling bank account.

Currency

Using ATMs with your debit card will get you a bad exchange rate from your bank, which I why I recommend a travel card like Revolut, and I still prefer ATMs to walking around with heaps of cash. I honestly try and keep cash to a minimum, obviously depending on how card-friendly your destination is. In my six weeks in South Africa, I only went to an ATM once and withdrew $100. For taxis, I used Uber, and I paid for everything else on my travel card. No chance to get mugged and lose lots of cash, no worrying about correct change or exchange rates... easy.

Be wary of anyone who approaches you at an ATM. First examine it for any obvious card-skimming devices and try to use one in a large mall or inside a bank. You're much less likely to get scammed. I once had my bank account fully cleaned out in Honduras after being forced by circumstance to use a dodgy-looking ATM. I desperately wished I'd planned ahead and made it to a proper bank. Fortunately, a call to the bank-of-dad helped me out, and I eventually claimed it on insurance. These days, I use a travel card so there is only a quite limited amount available at any one time, and I just top up as needed. It certainly saves me some worry. Some countries won't allow for their currency to be transferred back into dollars or euros, so don't be caught out; spend it all while you're there, before crossing the border.

Be aware of the tipping culture in the place you plan to visit. In some places it's expected, some gratefully received, and some downright rude to tip! Yes, we're travelling and trying to save money, but some people rely on tips to survive, and if you can't afford to tip in a fancy restaurant, should you be eating there in the first place?

Always make sure you have a little bit of emergency cash on you, enough to get you home in a taxi if push comes to shove. There's nothing worse than not having the money to get home or buy some tasty street food you see.

If you really feel the need to carry lots of cash or are going somewhere, they really do not accept cards (you'd be surprised at the tiny islands that do, nowadays), then shop around for a good exchange rate. Often money changers in big tourist hotspots offer a horrible rate to backpackers, knowing they will opt for convenience over sense. Be suspicious if anyone wants to change money for you at borders – there are lots of fake notes being handed out; it's better to use an official booth. Similarly, when you are getting change from any transaction, examine your notes, especially if they are large, and make sure they aren't phoney.

When you're exchanging money, wherever you are, it's sensible to work out first how much local currency you expect to get for the amount you're exchanging. That way, if the teller works it out wrong, you'll know straight away; once you walk away, it's your problem. Try and ask for small denominations of the currency; large ones are often difficult to spend. If you do have to pay with a large bill, make sure it is clear what you have given to the waiter or shopkeeper. Incorrect change and a denial of said large bill's existence happen more often than you think.

Any transaction involving medium-to-large amounts of money should put you on high alert. Any transaction involving your giving money to someone, and that person's going out of the room or down the road with your money to collect your purchase, should set off alarm bells and possibly a big, flashy, red light.

Be scam-conscious with fellow travellers, as well as with locals. If a fellow traveller needs money fast to get her out of trouble, why has she come to you rather than asking a friend or family member to wire her some? Has she contacted the local police, or the embassy? If not, why not? Be aware, be assertive, and you should be fine.

Nothing I can tell you will guarantee that you don't get scammed. There are as many scams as there are scamsters, and some are mighty cunning. I could tell you not to trust anyone you meet, but that wouldn't make for particularly fun travels. My best advice is this: don't be scared but be aware.

Money-saving Hacks

There are plenty of tips and tricks you can use to save money on the road, preserving your cash for the real experiences that matter. Here are my top 10.

1. Whether you see it as a fun part of travelling or a pain in the arse, haggling is a key part of shopping in many countries. If the price of an item is displayed clearly, haggling won't be necessary and might cause offence. If it isn't, then assume that the price of whatever you're buying is negotiable.

   As a buyer, it's impossible to find out how much items "should" cost. In countries without Watchdog and Which? magazine, there's simply no "should" about it. Shop around, talk to fellow travellers, and you won't get ripped off too badly. There's only one hard-and-fast rule when it comes to haggling, and that's to do it with good grace. Yes, the stallholder may be charging you five times more than he'd charge a local, but that's because, to him, you seem very rich. Your plane ticket to get to his country cost more than he'll earn in his lifetime, don't think he doesn't know this. Be assertive by all means, but be polite too, and above all, smile.

2. Go local when you can – think local food, local

transport, local anything you can! Not only will you get a more authentic experience, but you will have saved some money in the process.

3. Food and drink: If your hostel has a kitchen, a local supermarket can be an adventure, and communal cooking can be economical and a great way to make friends. Try knocking together a picnic for a day out without the price tag. Lunch in the sun is often its own treat.

For that occasional time you're craving a fancy feast, try going at lunchtime. There are often great deals at nice restaurants with the same high-quality food, or even check out Groupon if you're somewhere for a few days to grab a deal. If it's only occasional, a special treat meal out will feel exactly that, a treat, and a cocktail in a nice bar after having beers on the beach for a few days will be a special event. Try set menus for a big feed, you'll often save a bundle, and try not to eat out all the time.

Get to know your tap water. Often, we are forced to buy bottled water abroad, due to the differences in our digestive systems and the filtration standards not quite being up to western standard, but if you can drink the tap water, then do so! Fancy bottled water can be such a waste of money, especially at restaurants, if tap water will do the same job just fine!

4. Find some free stuff to do! Look what's going on in the area. Are there street fairs or carnivals? Watching the sunset or going to the beach are free, too, and still great experiences. Hiking can be a beautiful way to while away an afternoon, or see what free walking tours or free museums there are locally. You'd be surprised how much time you can spend doing free stuff if you try, leaving money for the days that have expensive activities.

5. Budget your time and not just your travel. There is nothing worse than rushing to the airport, bus terminal or train station because of the tardiness of checking out of a hostel, relying on another form of transportation, getting stuck in traffic, etc. Give yourself an extra hour or two, regardless of whether you feel it is needed on both ends (departing from one location and arriving at another). Poor time management can cost you greatly, especially if you had hopes of catching the last train to the airport, the last boat to the

mainland/island to make your hostel reservation, or worse. There will always be a Plan B available; just expect to pay four to ten times as much to make last-minute changes to transportation and/or accommodation arrangements.

6. You know that saying, "Collect moments, not things"? It's definitely true. While it may be tempting to collect small trinkets throughout your trip, these little expenses add up and also take precious space in your (probably heavy) bag. In my experience, the best souvenirs are free, like photos, ticket stubs, etc. Save money AND space by forgoing souvenirs; it's a win-win. Don't feel guilt-tripped into buying gifts for people back home. I really doubt they want a tribal pendant from the Amazon or a toy llama from Peru, and definitely not one of those infernal wooden ribbiting frogs from Thailand. Share your memories and photos when you get home and save your pennies.

7. Use the sharing economy to find cheaper accommodation, quirky tour guides, rideshare options and home-cooked meals with local chefs. You can bypass the traditional travel industry with sharing economy websites and

gain access to locals using their own assets and skills. Moreover, locals know where to find deals. They know which supermarket is cheapest, which stores offer the best deals and where to find the hole-in-the-wall restaurants and bars with the tastiest food at the lowest prices. Talking directly to them gives you access to that knowledge. Vayable.com is a favourite of mine.

8. Think! Always think before spending every penny: "Do I really need to buy this?", "Can I get this cheaper elsewhere?", "Would I rather spend this money on something else?", "Can I afford to do this in the long term?", "Can I go without?". Remember every little bit you save reduces the cost of travelling, and it all adds up. Even if you can manage to save just $1 here and there every day over a three-month trip, it adds up to $90, easily an extra week travelling in a country as cheap as Thailand.

9. Share. If you can share a taxi or a hotel room, you've just halved the price and doubled the fun. Making friends while travelling is easy, and you'll soon find like-minded people to split costs with.

10. Don't give up! Trying to stick to a travel budget

is hard work, but don't lose sight of your goal. After a few months on the road staying in basic accommodation, it can be very tempting to go out and splurge on a fancy hotel room and a five-course meal. To be honest, sometimes you deserve it. Just don't make it a regular occurrence. The longer I have been on the road, the more I appreciate how far I can stretch my money. Remember, you will never remember that great night's sleep in a $200-a-night hotel, but you sure will remember forking out only $10 on a room so you could spend $190 on a once-in-a-lifetime activity. Long-term travel is hard, and so is sticking to a budget. The rewards, however, are always worth it.

Long-term Travel Finance

If you're looking for a very extended trip or you love a place so much that you just want to stay, sometimes it's necessary to go to extreme measures to save money or generate income on your trip. Slowing down your travels to fully appreciate and live in a country can be so much more rewarding than skipping through it in days or weeks. Worry not, because there are plenty of ways to do this.

While the thought of working isn't necessarily a great one when you've just busted your ass to save for your trip, the good thing about travel jobs is that you can pick them up for just weeks at a time to supplement your income, and they tend to be low-stress and fairly fun.

The most obvious choices are bar or hostel work, but farm work is another great option for budget backpackers wanting to stretch their cash that bit further. Picking up a job on the road is usually as simple as just spending an afternoon asking around.

You can work at hostels, and in exchange for three to four hours' graft a day, you get free digs and often free beer. You will often find that backpacker jobs are not even like real jobs; they are so much more relaxed and informal that it doesn't even feel like work.

You can also find placements on sites like Workaway. You pay just $29 for the year and then have access to literally thousands of projects all around the world where you can help out in exchange for food and board. Generally, you do not need to be skilled to get placements on Workaway, but a positive attitude, common sense and a willingness to engage are a must. If you are planning long-term travel, this will help lower your costs significantly, particularly in more expensive destinations.

If you know you want to travel long term before you leave then consider what working visas you're eligible for. Australia, New Zealand, the UK and others have great programs that allow you to (legally) get a job and can help offset the cost of experiencing these amazing but expensive countries. It might take a bit of time and effort to apply for them, so get organised well in advance of your trip.

If you want something a bit more long-term, formal and better paying, then consider teaching English as a foreign language. A TEFL certificate can be obtained pretty easily and will enhance your employability tenfold. Personally, working as a scuba diving instructor has allowed me to live in eight different countries for varying lengths of time to top up my travel fund.

Also, consider house sitting as an easy way to extend your stay, especially in a big, expensive city where accommodation cost is a major factor. There are plenty of websites where you can register to do this. Build up your profile, and you can pick and choose your assignments. Looking after pets is often part and parcel of these gigs, but it's definitely a way to spend real time in a country and integrate yourself like a local, in accommodation that would be difficult to afford otherwise.

CHAPTER 10

TECHNOLOGY

It's amazing to think how different this section would have been if I had written it 10 years ago – if I'd have included it at all! But now technology is a huge part of our lives, and with the advent of super cheap and fast Wi-Fi and data services in even the most remote of locations, it can offer us a way to get so much more out of our travels.

When I first left home, the internet options consisted of dial-up connections in internet cafes at sometimes extortionate prices. Pre-typing emails offline and then logging on and sending them all at once was a trick I employed often. I remember making one phone call home for a special occasion, and it cost me $20. We have many more options now, so let's embrace them!

Your Phone

Make sure your phone is unlocked before you leave home, and buy a local SIM in each country. This offers great flexibility, and you never have to worry about i when you're out and about. They are cheap as chips; add a data plan and you're away. Take your passport when you buy a SIM; this is often required, to stop criminal communications.

If you are relying on Wi-Fi, most touristy cafes and restaurants have it, but just ask before you sit down. If you're in a fix, remember that almost every Starbucks and McDonalds in the world has free internet, and there's normally one of them close by!

Make sure you back up your phone regularly. The last thing you want is to lose all your pictures and new contacts by having your phone stolen. Find some reliable Wi-Fi every now and again and do a manual backup if it's not set to automatic. You'll thank yourself later.

Technology Trap

While all this new functionality is amazing and can enhance our travel lives immensely, there is a danger that we'll stop looking up from our screens and get absorbed in our online life. It makes me sad when, more and more regularly, I see stunning views and chances to interact missed by travellers mindlessly scrolling on Facebook. Make sure you look up from your phone and appreciate the amazing surroundings that you are in.

Photos

Unless you are a serious photographer with a big DSLR, you don't need a camera while travelling. Most phones are as good as point-and-shoot cameras these days, anyway, and it's just one more thing to carry around and look after. Plus it becomes a pain getting the pictures off to share them. Take time to take thoughtful and amazing photos; no one ever comes back from a trip wishing they'd taken fewer pictures! Lots of blurry pictures of drunken nights out aren't quite what you are going for here (but of course they have their place), but try and capture the amazing sights you see and people you meet.

If you're by yourself, don't be shy about asking others for help taking photos. Pretty views are nice, but it would be better to see you in some pictures too! Be sensitive when taking photos of locals. Ask permission first. Most are happy to oblige, but some people find it offensive if you start snapping away at them. If they ask you for money, walk away; there are plenty of other things to take snaps of!

Amazing Apps

There are literally thousands of apps you can download before you go that will help you on your way, and I'm sure that you will find your favourites if you take time to download a few and get familiar with them before you leave. Here are my top 20!

Logistics

1. HostelWorld: Browse and book your next bed on this easy-to-use app. Read reviews and great descriptions to match yourself to a hostel that suits your needs and fits your travel style. You can often even pay through the app before you arrive, making check-in hassle free. A must-have for those booking on the fly.

2. TripAdvisor: What are the best things to do, best places to eat? It can be overwhelming when you arrive in a new city. While I would take TripAdvisor with a pinch of salt (people are much more likely to post bad reviews than good ones), it can be a great starting point to learn what attractions you should be hitting up and what restaurants are a must-try.

3. TripIt: If you don't have time to create a detailed and organized travel itinerary, you should definitely download this app. All you need to do is forward the confirmation emails of your trip, stuff such as your hotel, flight and other reservations. TripIt will then automatically create a master itinerary for

your whole trip. It works offline, so once it's saved on your phone, you can access it anytime.

4. Rome2Rio: Being in the know about your transport options between destinations can save you a lot of time and money. This is seriously the most amazing app for finding out transportation connections, even in the most remote places. Type in where you are and where you're going, and you get a list of bus, train, flight and self-drive options.

5. Airbnb: If you are tired of staying in hotels or hostels and want to experience something different, Airbnb is a great option. Whether an apartment for a night, a castle for a week, or a villa for a month – Airbnb offers various types of accommodation that are hosted privately.

Getting Around

6. XE Currency: Always make sure you know how much you're paying and double check those money changers so you don't lose out! The best way to avoid getting overcharged abroad (or just making costly mistakes) is to have the latest exchange rates with you all the time. XE Currency doesn't need to be connected to the

internet to work; just make sure you load the currencies you need before you lose connection.

7. MAPS.ME: This is an awesome maps app that lets you download map data for a country or region so you can use it even when you have no data connection. This app was a serious lifesaver when I was trying to find my way through the infinite windy alleyways of the medina in Fez, Morocco – not to mention many other places! While Google Maps now also includes a downloading function, I like the Maps.me functionality better. It also lets you more easily star specific locations for later reference.

8. Google Maps: You need never get lost in a foreign place if you have Google Maps. It pinpoints your exact location, tells you how to get to your desired destination, and allows you to search for nearby hotels, restaurants and other establishments. It can act as a Satnav and keep you safe on taxi rides by following your route.

9. Google Translate: If you're on Android, you may already have this. Either way, get this app and add it to your home screen! Not only can you translate text by manually typing it in; it

can instantly translate a conversation or render translated text on top of a camera picture. Google recently switched to translations based on machine learning, making the results much better, especially for difficult translations like Japanese to English.

10. Uber: In busy cities like Bangkok or Manila, Uber is a godsend! While riding a tuk-tuk is fun and is a quintessential, I've-been-to-Asia-experience, most of the time, they try to rip you off. Save yourself the hassle of arguing rates. Instead, with a tap of your phone, you can call yourself an Uber to take you anywhere you want to go.

<u>Staying in Contact</u>

11. Skype: Skype video calls are a fantastic way to keep up with your friends or family back home. But it's also a great way to make cheap international voice calls! I've found this extremely useful in cases where I had to call the support desk of my bank or insurer while abroad. Just put a little credit in your Skype account, and you can call numbers in your home country at local tariffs.

12. WhatsApp: Whether you're instant messaging

people across the world or across the street, WhatsApp Messenger is the most popular messaging app in the world. People in countless countries use this app to message each other. With this app, you can also make voice and video calls, as well as send voice messages, pictures, gifs, documents and location information. One of the best things about WhatsApp is its powerful end-to-end encryption; everything you send and receive on WhatsApp is highly secure.

Entertainment

13. Netflix: For me, the download-for-later feature on my Netflix app has saved me from many a dull bus ride. While I don't recommend getting into the habit of series binging on the road (after all, you should be out enjoying yourself), now and again it can be just what you need.

14. Spotify: I have the Spotify premium account, which means I can download all my favourite tunes and playlists to listen to when there's no Wi-Fi or data to be found. I use the podcasts to death as well; for me, it's a great way to while away some time when I'm hiking or waiting to board a plane.

15. Scribd: Scribd is one of my all-time favourite apps. It's a bookstore, but, unlike similar competitors such as Audible, it lets you have an unlimited number of books for one flat monthly fee – like Netflix for books and audiobooks! With the amount I was spending on audiobooks and Kindle buys, this app is a godsend. When it's too bumpy (or I'm too lazy) to actually read, listening to audiobooks makes boring down-time zip by in a snap.

Backups

16. Google Drive: I have a file from my laptop synced to my phone, with all my important documents available in a flash. From photocopies of my passport to insurance details, even my CV has come in super handy when I've needed it. Get it uploaded before you go and give yourself a frustration-free life.

17. LastPass: This app saves all my passwords and credit/debit card info. It's super secure and can be a lifesaver if you get logged out of websites or have security alerts from being logged onto different computers. This has saved me so much agony when I have had my purse stolen or dropped my laptop bag into the murky water of the marina in Cape Town.

Fun

18. VOLO: It's fun to keep some kind of journal during your trip. While you could easily use the built-in notepad apps, it's more fun to use a dedicated travel journal app. With VOLO, you can create a kind of scrapbook, including pictures and text, and can even co-author your journey with your fellow travel buddies.

19. Piccolo: It's a fun, phone-based drinking game, perfect for breaking the ice in a new hostel or getting to know your new travel buds. It works offline, so you can use it anywhere. All you need is a few bevvies and a sense of humour.

20. VSCO: This simple-to-use photo-editing app can make your travel snaps Instagram-worthy in a snap. A few tweaks and a filter thrown in will scream "professional travel blogger" in no time!

SECTION 3

THE RETURN

The days have slowly ticked by, the bank account has dwindled and your wrist is heavy with the weight of the tens of manky bracelets adorning it. It's time to go home.

Coming home after travelling can be weirdly jarring. There are all these things you became used to while you were away, and now you're back, you just can't get back to reality. Making the return to normal life is not something that should be brushed aside as "easy". You should treat it as carefully as you did preparing for your travels to ensure you don't end up in a reverse culture shock nightmare.

There's nothing wrong with going home, although most travellers find themselves a little altered, with new perspectives, skills and attitudes. It's ok to be different now. Wasn't that the point of going travelling in the first place?

CHAPTER 11

SETTLING BACK HOME

First Steps

Give yourself a break! The list of things you have to do when you get back can be overwhelming. Getting over jet-lag, catching up with everyone, reading unopened mail, finding a job, an apartment, dentist appointments... the list is seemingly endless.

Take a breath, and breathe for a few days. If things have waited months to be done, they can wait a few more days. Don't exhaust yourself with rushing around. Just sleep, unpack, schedule a few (not loads) of social activities to wean yourself back in and give your body a chance to readjust to time zones, climate differences and diet. There's no rush, and the only pressure is that which you put on yourself. Give yourself a few days' grace before you start on the fast track again.

Make a list of the things you need to do to restart your home life and put them in order. Tackle a few easy ones first to get the ball rolling and then prioritise them in order of need. If you have a bit of a buffer fund to get you through the first few weeks, then great, it takes the pressure off finding a job so you can relax and readjust at your own pace.

Make sure you take care of any health concerns you had on the road and readjust any naughty drinking or eating habits that may have developed. They often sneak in when we're away; just don't let them infiltrate your home environment. Try and pick up the routines you had before you left, like hitting the gym or taking vitamins. It will make you feel back to your old self again a little more quickly.

Post Trip Blues

I have often found the first week or so of returning home amazingly easy. You have so many friends to meet up with and are excited about novelties like hair straighteners and your favourite foods or clothes. When these topics are exhausted and the quiet humdrum of life at home starts to dawn on me is when I start to totter downhill.

It is week two that I plan for, and I have to use all the tips and tricks in my arsenal to not sink into the darkness. Here's my foolproof, step-by-step plan towards a successful transition home.

1. Get in a routine. It will seem alien, as for the last few months you've been adjusting to not having any routine at all. But getting back into the swing of things back home is essential, and a strong routine will help you adjust. Set a normal waking up time and stick to it. Same with going to bed: staying up all night watching Netflix and sleeping through the morning will not help you crush the day. Try and fit in with "normal" people and routines. Even if you don't have a job just yet, act as if you do. Conduct the job hunt from nine to five, and you'll feel satisfied after the day. This might mean polishing your CV, meeting with recruitment agencies or doing the rounds looking for casual work. Try and fit your usual evening activities back into place. Did you use to go to yoga on Tuesdays or meet friends on Thursday nights? Structure is the key to not looking at Instagram all day, day-dreaming about beach-side cocktails.

2. Keep the travel attitude. Now you have all the new skills, they don't have to be packed away with your backpack. Go off on adventures, see your local town, explore new restaurants solo, meet new people by striking up conversations in bars. You did it while away, who says you

can't do it back at home? Why is it that when you're abroad, you'll do things you'd never dream of doing back home? Like bungy jumping or mountain biking. If it made you feel so good, why stop now? So, book a paragliding session, climb a mountain or join an aerial yoga class if you want to.

3. Seek a new challenge. If you find yourself with lots of free time and a yearning to do something, try and channel it into something useful. Why not learn to play the guitar, study the language you picked up the basics of or take an online course in something that interests you? Setting yourself a new goal will distract you from travel daydreams and pour your free time into something you can feel good about achieving.

4. Take time out. One of the most enjoyable things about long-term travelling is having time to please yourself. Whole days spent lying in a hammock or exploring a town... So, at home make time for self-indulgence, too. Relax with a book in the sun, while away an afternoon in a café with your laptop and a coffee or take yourself off to a quirky museum that only you would be interested in.

5. Stay in touch with your travel friends. I'm always in two minds about Facebook, but it can be a godsend for keeping in touch and up-to-date with people when they live on the other side of the world. Make an effort to arrange a Skype call or send messages to those special people you met travelling. They are the ones that shared your experiences and the ones that understand how you're feeling. A little catch-up and a giggle about shared memories can be so refreshing in your home life and remind you why you went to all that bother in the first place.

6. Read your journal and look at your photos (but not too much!). Take some time to scroll back through your snaps and remember all the amazing times you had. Get your favourites printed out so you can have them on your wall and reminisce. If you bothered to keep a travel journal, this is where it pays you back tenfold, recreating those feelings and transporting you back into moments in time. Just make sure you're not obsessing about the past. It's great to look back, not so great to spend hours a day wishing for something that's not your current reality.

7. Don't be a travel bore: "When I was in Dubai…" and "These kale crisps aren't a patch on the deep-fried locusts I ate in Myanmar." Oh how easily the nostalgic phrases trip off the tongue. You wish you could stop. You've become a traveller parody, and you know it. Even so, it's frustrating when you've just had some life-changing experiences and no-one seems remotely interested. One way around this is to write a travel blog. You'll get all the stories out of your system, plus all your friends and family can share the adventure while you're living it – and it's up to them if they choose to read it. This means that when you come home, you can relax and enjoy hearing other people's stories rather than bombarding them with recollections. While your friends and family at home want to hear stories about your adventures and see your pictures, be careful about overdoing it. Make sure you don't go on about how bad it is being back home. After all, they have chosen to live there! While it's important to share, no want wants to hear how much better it was in Budapest or how much friendlier it is in Costa Rica. Know your audience.

8. Think of the positives of being home, because

there are loads. While travelling is an amazing experience, there are so many aspects to it that are annoying, uncomfortable and frustrating. Now you can appreciate having personal space, more possessions, no tricky currency or time zone conversions, no language barriers or getting lost, your taken-for-granted safety and security. Remember that travelling wasn't always a laugh a minute. What about the time your bag got nicked along with your passport and bank cards? How does your bedroom compare with that dorm in the hostel from hell? Then there was getting lost in a town with incomprehensible street signs, and being scammed the minute you stepped off the plane... Now that you're home, getting things done is miraculously easy; trips to the bank and the doctor are a breeze. Depending on where you've returned from, the pavements may seem exceptionally clean, the roads much safer, and, joy of joys, there's decent Wi-Fi. Buying food is also straightforward; you don't have to barter, and it's unlikely you'll accidentally buy chickens' feet.

9. Make the most of the ways you've changed. Surviving all sorts of difficult situations, from

dodgy scams to hellish bus journeys, gives you confidence in your ability to look after yourself. If you found work in unlikely places, you'll know you can do it again back home (even if it's just any old job, for now). You met all sorts of people, from the lovely to the nutty, so your relationship skills can only have improved. Plus, you're now so laidback that you see the morning rush hour as an opportunity for valuable thinking time. And it's amazing how your new budgeting skills can stretch a dollar!

10. Realise how lucky you are. Not everyone gets to travel. So instead of moping about the house, take a moment to consider this and keep hold of the memories of a trip that made your life that bit richer. You have stories to tell the grandchildren about things that wouldn't be worth telling if you did them every day.

11. Start planning your next trip! This can be as simple as a weekend away to visit an old friend or a full-blown, round-the-world adventure. If you have a plan or a goal, it can be much easier to stay focused on what you have to do to get there. Maybe you could work abroad in a country you fell in love with? Or maybe it's

time to start saving up again to visit somewhere new on your bucket list. A dream is enough to pull you through the now.

Reverse Culture Shock

To me, reverse culture shock is difficult to explain if you have never experienced it. How different can one culture really be to another? As it turns out, it can be vastly different! From food to religion, family values, music, TV, high street shops, markets and clothes, everything is different in some way. Everything we see, hear and feel influences our culture, and our culture influences how we see the world and conduct ourselves in it.

Feeling like a stranger in your own country is bizarre, but it needn't be a bad thing. Reverse culture shock symptoms can range from irritability to stress and depression, but don't rush; give yourself time to adjust to your new old surroundings. Travel changes your perspective on everything, but it also makes you more open-minded and adaptable to change, even when you go back. Keep some memories of your travels, but don't dwell on the past. Reconnect with the people you missed while you were away, friends, family and loved ones; they are a unique adventure too!

People always talk about travelling to find themselves, but in the process, you'll likely lose a lot of what you thought you knew about yourself. When we travel, we see so many different ways of living, which can challenge any ideas we might previously have had about how we wanted to live our lives. So if you plan a backpacking trip as a minor detour on your carefully paved life path, don't be surprised if you return home to find that path a bit bumpier, overgrown, or split in twelve.

The first time I came back home from an extended trip, it was as if home had remained frozen during my time away. I still loved my friends, family and city, but I realized I didn't fit in anymore. I had outgrown living there. Home felt small and unrelatable. I had this fire in me that I couldn't express to anyone, and it frustrated me. I yearned to try new things, go new places and meet new people, but whenever I tried to express that, my words fell flat. That fire was a feeling only those who had travelled seemed to grasp; a simple nod conveyed an understanding of this shared bond. When I talked to my friends, they brushed it off. To my parents, it was as if I was equivocating on my place of birth.

As the excitement of home wore off, I wondered what was next. I was restless. I felt stale. Did I take this long trip only to end up right back where I started? No, of course not. I took it to grow as a person.

It's always great to catch up with my friends when I get back, and we have all changed, as you would expect. Marriages, mortgages and children have been most of their stories for the past few years, which I still can't imagine undertaking. We are still friends but have less and less in common as we spend less time together and prioritize different things. This is no bad thing, though, and I would expect no different. We all grow up, so perhaps it is me who is stuck in the past? Am I still clinging to the Peter Pan-like existence, backpacking with twenty-year-olds despite being into my thirties? Do my friends think I'm crazy or are they a little jealous? Do I think they are crazy or am I a little jealous? Perhaps it is all of the above.

As Benjamin Button said, "It's a funny thing about comin' home. Looks the same, smells the same, feels the same. You'll realize what's changed is you." Coming home is easier now than it was that first time in 2006, but the road still beckons me after just a few days. I know it's there that I will find kindred spirits who understand me and the adventure I seek. It's where I find like-minded people who also broke out of the Matrix.

When we're all hugged out, the stories told and the

reunions over, many of us find that coming back home isn't really coming home at all. Our true home is being surrounded by the unknown. The road is where we belong. And because of that, our gaze will always be on the horizon, looking, dreaming and doing what we do best: wishing (and plotting) for another opportunity to get away again.

ABOUT THE AUTHOR

Victoria grew up on the outskirts of London and left home straight after graduating from school. She has hardly stayed still since. Becoming a scuba diving instructor at 18 allowed her to travel the world while working, using any spare time and money backpacking the far-flung corners of the globe.

After attending university to gain a business degree, she spent two years forcing herself into a fancy financial consulting job in the city but soon re-joined the realms of the restless and moved to the Caribbean to continue blowing bubbles.

Currently working as a scuba instructor on a superyacht, she now teaches diving to the rich and famous.

Victoria has lived in eight different countries and has travelled to 83 more and counting. She still has a long bucket list.

ONE LAST THING...

If you've enjoyed this book or found it useful, I'd be very grateful if you could post a short review on Amazon. Your support really does make a difference, and I read all your reviews personally so I can make this book even better.

Thanks again for your support!

Happy travels...

Printed in Great Britain
by Amazon